A Chronicle of Jails

CLASSICS OF IRISH HISTORY
General Editor: Tom Garvin

Some Recent Titles
Original publication dates of reprinted titles are given in brackets

A Chronicle of Jails

DARRELL FIGGIS

with an introduction by William Murphy

UNIVERSITY COLLEGE DUBLIN PRESS
Preas Choláiste Ollscoile Bhaile Átha Cliath

First published in Dublin by Talbot Press, 1917
This edition published by University College Dublin Press, 2010
Introduction © William Murphy, 2010

ISBN 978-1-906359-30-0
ISSN 1393–6883

University College Dublin Press
Newman House, 86 St Stephen's Green
Dublin 2, Ireland
www.ucdpress.ie

Cataloguing in Publication data available from the British Library

Introduction typeset in Scotland in Ehrhardt by Ryan Shiels
Text design by Lyn Davies, Frome, Somerset, England
Printed in England on acid-free paper by
CPI Antony Rowe, Chippenham

CONTENTS

ABBREVIATIONS

BMH	Bureau of Military History
IRB	Irish Republican Brotherhood
NA	National Archives
NAI	National Archives of Ireland
NLI	National Library of Ireland
RAMC	Royal Army Medical Corps
RIC	Royal Irish Constabulary
TNA	The National Archives
2RN	Radio News 2

INTRODUCTION

William Murphy

Books, glory be. A man once saw something for himself, and he wrote a book about it. The book wasn't the thing he saw by a mighty long measure, you may be sure; just because he thought more of himself writing it than the thing he saw. . . . Some other bright lad read that book, and he wrote another. Likely enough, a number of bright lads wrote books. And then the world was started in on the business. Books came out on top of books. Books were the children and fathers of books. . . . Great fellows rose up looking wise, and silly people gave them respect; and why? Because they wrote books saying that other people had written books; and what they had written in those books; when they were born; what women they married; and when they died. . . . That's what books have brought us. ... The world is moidhered with books.[1] (Darrell Figgis, 1922)

Sometime in the early months of 1917 Darrell Figgis wrote a short book. In the preface he promised to provide 'a record . . . set down with some care and faithfulness' of his arrest and internment in the aftermath of the 1916 Rising and he called it *A Chronicle of Jails*. The book's structure seems to confirm the disavowal of affectation and superfluity that Figgis insinuates in his preface and in his title. Figgis's itinerary of incarceration was in many ways typical of a 1916 internee and he guides us through this. Beginning in a provincial Irish prison and moving to the clearing house of Richmond

Barracks in Dublin, he was deported to England, to Stafford Jail. On leaving Stafford, Figgis's experience departed from the norm. Instead of joining the great majority of internees at Frongoch Camp in north Wales, Figgis was held in Reading Jail where the authorities sent those internees they considered 'the leaders of the Sinn Féiners'.[2] Like all internees, he was taken on a brief summer trip to London to appear before a committee chaired by Sir John Sankey. Sankey and his colleagues reviewed each case and recommended the release of 1,273 of the 1,846 internees they interviewed, but Darrell Figgis was not among these. Instead, he was forced to await the unconditional general release of the remaining internees which came in the days before Christmas 1916. All this Figgis charts, in a detail which is useful for the historian, and in a style which is often enjoyable to read, although when writing *A Chronicle* he often thought, and revealed, 'more of himself writing it than the thing he saw'.

I

To suggest that Darrell Figgis thought, talked, and wrote about himself a great deal is not a new charge. Edward Bulfin, who was interned at Durham Prison with Figgis in 1918, described him as 'the Sacred Egoist'.[3] Much later, in 1939, when Figgis was long dead, Padraic Colum contributed a portrait of the man he knew to the *Dublin Magazine*. Colum's assessment was sympathetic in many ways, but he too emphasised this aspect of Figgis's personality:

> But he was an unaccountable man, Darrell Figgis; one of the most unaccountable men I ever knew. Outwardly, he was candid, amiable, companionable; inwardly, he was self-centred to an astonishing degree. He was a man who could be counted on to do a dangerous thing, and he was a man who, having done that thing, would be endlessly loquacious about it.[4]

This is not the place to give a full account of the life and death of Darrell Figgis, but the failures and tragedies of his final years have cemented the image of a peculiarly egotistical man, colouring all that he did before and all that has been written of him since. Although he was sporadically prominent in Irish public life in the years 1913 to 1925, he was a marginal figure. Such prominence as he attained did not depend on alliances or friendships; he had few of these as he 'lay out from every pack'.[5] Instead, he relied upon his talents as a writer and propagandist, his somewhat less certain capabilities as an administrator, the fact that he had taken a central role in the Howth gun-running of July 1914, the significant patronage of Arthur Griffith, and his own undoubted talents for self-promotion. His unusual name did not harm him even when it attracted abuse: T. J. Condon, MP, asked a United Irish League rally in July 1917 if they wanted 'Darrell Figgis – he didn't know whether he pronounced it right or not, it was certainly not a Dalcassian name – instead of John Redmond', while M. Conway said of Sinn Féin at a similar event later that year that 'Their standard bearer, de Valera, was the son of a Spanish father; Darrell Figgis, their secretary, was the son of a Greek mother. The Sinn Feiners were not quite right; they all had some kink in their character; they were not rational men, like the plain sons of the old sod of Ireland.'[6]

In the years after independence, however, he became ever more marginalised. Firstly, he ran as an independent pro-Treaty candidate rather than on the joint platform at the pact election of June 1922, provoking the ire of many in both the pro- and anti-Treaty factions. With days to go to polling a group of republicans forced their way into his apartment and shaved off half of his beard. Then Griffith, perhaps the only leading political figure in the new state who saw Figgis's attributes before he saw Figgis's kinks, died. Worse was to follow; Figgis became the subject of scandal as a consequence of an association with a businessman named Andrew

Belton. Although Figgis had little enough influence to sell, one of Belton's companies briefly paid Figgis a salary in return for the alleged access he could afford Belton, who hoped to obtain various government contracts and licences. The arrangement, which had lasted several months in 1922 before ending in rancour, was revealed in 1924. Then Belton was among those lobbying for a contract to run the Irish Free State's first radio station and Figgis was a member of a Dáil committee established to report on the issue. It was Belton who exposed the relationship to the minister charged with the area of broadcasting, the Postmaster General, J. J. Walsh, because he feared that a bitter residue of the former connection would lead Figgis to impede his company's chances. In the event Belton succeeded in ruining his company's hopes and destroying Figgis's brittle reputation.[7]

If 1924 began with political humiliation it ended with personal tragedy. On 18 November his wife Millie, to whom *A Chronicle* was dedicated as 'The Lady at the Gate', killed herself. She hired a taxi cab from Shelbourne Motor Company, asking to be driven to the Hell Fire Club Tea Rooms, but on reaching Willbrook in Rathfarnham she shot herself in the back of the cab. In the minutes before she committed suicide her last, ambiguous, words to Robert Kerr, the driver, were 'This will be on account of my husband, Mr Darrell Figgis; remember that'. At the inquest Figgis explained that he had an account with the Shelbourne Motor Company and suggested that his wife's last words referred to this. 'Millie,' he explained, 'had been in a state of anxiety since the "Black and Tan" days' and particularly since the raid on their home in 1922. He produced and read to the inquest an alleged (bloodstained) suicide note which supported this thesis. The jury's sole task was to adjudicate on the immediate causes of death – 'shock and hemorrhage, due to a bullet wound self-inflicted while she was temporarily insane',[8] they decided – and the veracity of Figgis's explanation was not publicly challenged, but later events cast serious doubts on its credibility.

Less than a year later, on 22 October 1925, Figgis appeared as a key witness before another inquest. On this occasion, at Hendon Town Hall, Middlesex, he offered a plausible, but unconvincing, explanation of his role in the death of his lover, Rita North, aged twenty-one, a 'dancing mistress', from Thomas Street, Dublin. The immediate cause of her death was an infection that followed what the police suspected to be a botched abortion. In his statement to the inquest Figgis admitted 'I knew the deceased for about some-what more than two years'. He did not deny his paternity of Rita North's child, but did deny all knowledge of the pregnancy until, he insisted, an already ill Rita travelled from Dublin to seek his assistance at his London club on 5 October. Two weeks later, she died at Hendon Cottage Hospital, despite two operations intended to remove infection. The inquest was adjourned, but when it resumed on 5 November Figgis was not available to clarify his evidence. On the morning of 27 October a maid had discovered his body in a gas-filled room that he had rented at 4 Grenville Street in the Bloomsbury district of London. Like Millie, he had committed suicide.[9]

II

In the summer of 1917 Darrell Figgis did not live in the expectation of disgrace; then he had good reason to believe that he was a coming man. At thirty-four he had published three collections of poetry, three books of literary criticism, two novels and his play, *Queen Tara*, had been professionally staged at the Gaiety Theatre.[10] Although Figgis was born in Rathmines in 1882, the foundations of his literary career were built in London from 1909 where he wrote for various periodicals and acted as a literary agent for the publishers Dent & Sons. He had quit the family tea business, for which he had worked since his teens, to pursue the life of a writer and it was a combination of a desire to write about Ireland and an interest in Irish nationalism that brought him back to his native land around 1913.[11] He had made a mark in advanced nationalist circles and, if he wished to progress further in that arena, he had had the good fortune to be arrested in the aftermath of the Rising, although he had taken no active part whatsoever. His name had again come before the public in February 1917 when he was one of a group of activists arrested and deported. This time he was not dispatched to prison, but to a more salubrious exile in Oxford. It was probably while there that he wrote most of *A Chronicle*, before disobeying his deportation order in May and returning to Ireland.[12] In May 1917 Sinn Féin was on the rise and nationalist Ireland was abuzz at the victory in the South Longford by-election of a 1916 convict still held at Lewes Prison, Joe McGuinness, on the slogan 'Put him in to get him out'.[13]

Figgis concluded *A Chronicle* by describing the moment when he and his fellow internees 'passed out' of Reading Gaol to freedom, stating that as each man left the prison he 'remembered his fellows who still were in jail, the men who, for the same duty and for the same high cause, were serving sentences at Lewes'.[14] With great perspicacity or great fortune, the Talbot Press released Figgis's memoir to coincide with the British government's decision to release these convicts. On 15 June 1917 parliament was informed of the convicts' imminent amnesty[15] and on the following day the national newspapers in Ireland began to carry advertisements for *A Chronicle*.[16] In the days that followed the amnesty announcement, large crowds gathered at the North Wall and at Westland Row train station in Dublin in anticipation of the convicts' arrival. Nationalist Ireland wanted to see and touch the prisoners of 1916 and if Figgis and The Talbot Press had any luck then nationalist Ireland would want to read about the prisoners of 1916 (even if Figgis's experience differed from those who had served sentences as convicts). On the morning of 18 June the freed convicts finally arrived at Westland Row station to an enormous reception and on the same morning the *Irish Independent* recommended *A Chronicle* to its readers in a succinct but positive review.[17]

Rarely then has a prison memoir issued into a more receptive atmosphere. It seems to have sold well, at least for a time. As early as 7 July 1917 the *Irish Times* carried a further advertisement from The Talbot Press promising that a second edition was 'now ready'.[18] *A Chronicle* received further publicity in the *Irish Book Lover* where the reviewer praised Figgis's 'practised pen' and 'polished style',[19] and the book certainly did not hinder his election as secretary of the reorganised Sinn Féin in October 1917; however, it passed quickly into obscurity. In this it shared the fate of all the prison literature produced during the revolutionary period, including Figgis's subsequent volume, *A Second Chronicle of Jails*, which described his further internment in 1918 and 1919.[20] None of the many prison or internment camp memoirs produced during that era (and there were many) have joined the works of Mitchel, O'Donovan Rossa, or Davitt, in the pantheon of Irish prison classics. If prison writings featured prominently among the popular, nationalist classics to emerge from the Fenian era,[21] then the accounts of the revolutionary period which have consistently held the attention of the Irish public focused on the guerrilla fighter. Figgis, W. J. Brennan-Whitmore or Louis J. Walsh might have expected the ear of posterity, but it turned instead to Dan Breen, Tom Barry and Ernie O'Malley.[22]

This pattern is reflected in the outputs of those of us who read books and then try to write another. During the past fifteen years historians have offered much that is original and insightful about the organisation and activities of the Irish Volunteers and although we have not ignored political imprisonment during the Irish revolution, the world is not yet 'moidhered' with books on the subject. In the best academic study of Irish political prisoners to appear to date, Seán McConville provides a strong account of the efforts of the Home Office in Britain and the English Prison Commission to manage the Irish political prisoners thrust upon them due to violence or the threat of violence in Ireland between 1916 and 1921. Both of Figgis's prison memoirs are cited by McConville, but an extensive evaluation of their worth lay outside his book's remit.[23] Those few literary critics who have championed Figgis as a writer of substance have reserved their highest praise for his later novels and have treated his prison chronicles as minor, if admirable, aspects of his oeuvre. In dismissing Figgis's political pamphlets, journalism and memoirs, Robert Burnham did concede that his 'two short "Jail Chronicles" do possess an eloquent simplicity',[24] while Maryanne Wessel-Felter described the same works as 'powerful and effective pieces of autobiography/history that give a poignant as well as an important account of life in prison for the Irish patriots' before moving on to afford his fiction much greater attention.[25]

III

Unlike other memoirists among the 1916 internees who produced books in the immediate aftermath of their release,[26] Figgis was a professional writer. This influenced the shape and tone of his memoir. In *A Chronicle* it was important to him that he established his literary credentials early on; on the first page he informs us that he had spent the spring of 1916 working on a book that was late for the publishers, while later he tells us that when he fell ill at Stafford a sergeant in the Royal Army Medical Corps (RAMC) informed him that 'it had been discovered that I had written a book on Shakespeare, and that I was to be treated with respect accordingly'.[27] More importantly, the reader is immediately aware of Figgis's writerly aspirations when faced with his sentences; sentences that veer between the well honed and the over wrought. In describing the confusion of speculation on Achill Island during Easter week he wrote with directness and subtlety that 'The air was thick with rumours: rumours that were contradicted as soon as they came', but when explaining that in Richmond Barracks the prisoners were forced to sleep on the floor, in their own clothes, he could not resist the awful, 'It was extra-ordinary how soon one's hip-bones hardened to the floor and the simplicity of toilet was a great boon to anyone who had found dressing and undressing labyrinths of inconvenience.'[28] It was surely the desire to appear like a writer as well as be one, which is evidenced in the latter sentence, that prompted Brinsley MacNamara to warn a friend with literary pretensions that if he did not change his approach he would fall into 'the abysmal pitfall of premature vanity from which you might recover only after you had made yourself an absurd buffoon of literature or language like Figgis'.[29]

Figgis was atypical of Irish political prisoner memoirists of this period in that he acknowledged Oscar Wilde's 'Ballad of Reading Jail' as an inspiration. He makes reference to, and quotes from, Wilde's poem on several occasions, particularly towards the end of the memoir when Figgis too inhabits Reading's prison. Early in the memoir, Figgis describes being exercised alone in a small yard at Castlebar Prison. In the middle of the yard he finds two daisies which he picks before instantly regretting 'the selfishness and vandalism of the deed' because the daises are the only colour in a world of dark slate, flint floors and grey walls. Later, in Stafford, when briefly housed in the infirmary, he takes delight in an unusual blanket: 'Its colours were green, claret, and yellow. It lay on my bed like a spread cockatoo. Life could not be drab with that to look upon.' These moments are building towards his description of the exercise yard at Reading where the 'familiar asphalt paths could not be seen where they threaded their way amid the blossoms. In beds beneath the walls tall flowers lifted their heads, and even the graves of hanged men could not be seen beneath the blooms that covered

them.' This 'miracle' had been brought about by the prison authorities in response to Wilde's poem where he imagined roses instead
of 'the shard, the pebble, and the flint' because 'flowers have been
known to heal/A common man's despair'.[30]

Of course, Figgis drew not only on the 'Ballad of Reading Jail'
but on an established genre, even a tradition, of political prisoner
writings.[31] In noting that the internees 'were treading a path that
had already been sung (for even bitterness has its song)', Figgis had
Wilde in mind, but he also echoed Seán Milroy who wrote of his
time in Mountjoy Prison in 1915, 'the path I am treading is no longer
the ring of Mountjoy merely. It is the pathway of Irish history. ... I
hear the chains which O'Donovan Rossa drags after him.'[32] The
Talbot Press promoted *A Chronicle* as a 'Modern Jail Journal'[33] and
retailers such as the Fountain Book Shop in Cork, which marketed
itself as 'Run by Gaels for Gaels', listed it next to Mitchel's and
Milroy's memoirs in their advertisements.[34] The memoir is stocked
with the commonplaces of the genre; the shock as the cell door
shuts behind him for the first time, the sketch of the geography of
his cell, his swift acquisition of 'prison craft', the system's tendency
to erase the individual: 'In Stafford I was C 2:21: – Wing C, Balcony
2, Cell 21.'[35] Like other Irish political prisoners, however, Figgis
represents the collective experience of imprisonment as a moment
of rebirth. His Reading is also a 'university of revolution'.

For Figgis the great danger and the apparent purpose of prison
was the reduction of the prisoner to such a 'slow and sluggish' state
that incrementally he ceased to exist as a unique individual. He
insists that while in effective solitary confinement in the period that
followed his arrival at Stafford he experienced a 'dulling of the
consciousness, a blunting of the susceptibilities' and the onset of a
'blankness of being that it was the first duty of the whole system to
achieve'. He describes his attempts to prompt his mind to activity
by trying to imagine what his friends were doing at home, but 'at

most the wheel only spun around, never gripping the metal; and more often the wheel refused to move'.[36] In almost all the surviving detailed accounts by 1916 internees, including many of the recently released Bureau of Military History (BMH) statements, the first weeks after their removal from Ireland are recalled as the most difficult. Then, the internees were held alone in their cells for as many as twenty-three and three-quarter hours a day while a brief period of shared exercise was conducted in silence.[37] It seems likely that Figgis's description of that period and regime is largely based on the accounts he heard from colleagues who arrived at Stafford before him, as he did not leave Richmond Barracks until 23 May and the regime at Stafford was ameliorated within days of that date.

Like his colleagues, Figgis describes the relief, comfort and motivation that were to be found when the prison experience was shared rather than solitary. Of the overcrowded Richmond Barracks he writes that the hardships experienced there were mere 'campaigning inconveniences' whereas the 'great thing was that we were, by necessity, permitted one another's company'. In these circumstances began, he claims, 'a cementing of brotherhood'; at a distance the prisoners were 'chiefly aware of our differences from one another; but now that we came near one another we could see that our roots were in the same soil'. Even when in solitary at Stafford, everybody went to Mass on Sunday (including Protestants like Figgis) and there 'the body of song was a joy to hear after our enforced silence'. In Reading the select group held there, which varied in number from twenty-five to forty, revelled in an 'opportunity of meeting and understanding one another such as we never could have hoped for'.[38] He does, however, imply that prison did not always draw the internees closer together. The blessing of each others' company, he admits, 'might conceivably have been blurred a little, as with the passage of months it became difficult in our cramped space to avoid treading on one another's toes'[39] and, he concedes, they differed in the extent to which they withheld recognition from the Sankey Committee. In this matter he hints that his own lengthy hearing before the Committee was a matter of controversy and suspicion between his colleagues and himself, but suggests that his explanations – that he wanted to debate the legality of their detention and try to discover what allegations the police had made against him – were accepted.

In his representation of his relations with his fellow prisoners in *A Chronicle*, or rather in his failure to fully represent these relations, Figgis seems disingenuous or lacking in awareness. Figgis seemed to tread on more toes than anyone else as his 'gift, or curse, of attracting attention to himself' and his 'unusual facility for making enemies'[40] were magnified in the confined environment of the prison. When sent to Birmingham Prison in 1918, Peadar Ó hAnnracháin celebrated because, unlike in 1916, he was held in a different prison to Figgis. At least, he wrote to Henry Dixon, he need not 'fear the wrath of Darrell, because my black stockings would not get a chance of imprinting their shade on his immaculate léine [shirt]'.[41] Ernest Blythe claimed that he refused to swear Figgis into the IRB while at Reading because he had come 'to the conclusion that Figgis was no good', although, he admitted, that Griffith seemed to admire Figgis, perhaps because of Figgis's tendency to confront the prison authorities.[42] In Stafford Figgis had pushed himself to the fore as the prisoners' spokesman, but when he tried to do this at Reading the others were not enthusiastic, quickly installing Blythe in the position. Blythe was chosen so that Figgis could not attribute his demotion to his Protestantism.[43] This was a sensitive area. In *A Chronicle* Figgis insists that his Protestantism was not an issue. While in Stafford, he explains, he and other Protestant prisoners had joined their 'fellows in prayer to the one God'. However, Eamonn O'Duibhir, who was more sympathetic to Figgis than most witnesses, remembered that at Reading Figgis's attitude to prayers did cause some minor friction. Apparently, there the five Protestants among the prisoners again joined in general prayers convened each night just before lights out, but when Figgis knelt on a chair, rather than on the floor like everyone else, he drew down the wrath of his fellow Protestants.[44]

If they read it, there are passages in *A Chronicle* which must have drawn a wry smile from those colleagues who believed Figgis had an inflated opinion of his own influence. Early on, as news of the Rising breaks, Figgis records the worry of a friend that this event will spoil the progress that had been made just as the 'whole country was coming round to our way of thinking, business men and responsible men everywhere were waking up with your financial agitation and other things'.[45] Only Figgis or a friend could have vested such hopes in his influence upon the country. In his account of Stafford, Figgis is transparently proud that, in his own mind at least, he became someone who others followed and someone who bettered the conditions for his colleagues. He describes a day in the exercise yard at Stafford when he stepped out of the trudging file of men and 'began running easily within the circle that the others made about me'. The sergeant in charge looked on sceptically, but did not intervene and, according to Figgis, then 'another stepped out, and ran behind me; and another, and yet another' till this innovation became accepted practice.[46] If Figgis is to be believed, when at first the chaplain at Stafford, Fr Moore, was hostile it was Figgis who challenged him. As a consequence Moore's attitude was transformed and he 'moved among us intimately and always'. From Figgis's perspective, his complaints to the governor at Stafford influenced the onset of ameliorated conditions for the internees in late May. It is perhaps understandable that while in prison Figgis's field of vision narrowed to his own actions within the sealed environment of Stafford, but afterwards he must have become aware that it was unlikely this change in policy had a complaint from prisoner C

2:21 at its root.[47] Perhaps it was the knowledge that he was an outsider, distrusted by his colleagues, that impelled Figgis to trumpet his contributions to the cause in a manner that appeared self-centred and gauche. Whatever the reasons, this had the effect of confirming his marginality.

IV

An important impulse behind *A Chronicle* is, of course, propa-gandistic. British authority in Ireland is represented as heavy handed, capricious, and inept. Figgis describes the impact of the executions and wholesale arrests that followed the Rising as inducing a mood that moved from 'sullenness . . . to exasperation'. He mocks the arrival at his house, in the dead of night, of 'eighteen peelers, three sergeants, and a district inspector' to take him from his wife, eight hens and fifteen chickens.[48] He paints a picture of a society 'elaborately policed' by what Ernie O'Malley referred to as the 'the antennae . . . and the globose eye'[49] of the RIC, but ridicules the apparent absence of logic or justice governing consequent decisions to arrest, intern, court martial or release. He recounts the chief warder's warning at Castlebar that 'Rules don't apply now. Nothing applies. ... They might take you out to-morrow morning and shoot you so they might, and nobody to save you.'[50] The sense that in being arrested he had become subject to an arbitrary, confused and sometimes cruel power, and the anxiety this engendered, is com-municated through small incidents more often than mortal threats. He recounts that while still at Castlebar he wrote to his wife, assur-ing her that he would send a daily letter as a sign that he was safe, only to find his right to send such a letter suddenly withdrawn. He alleges that the authorities effected his deportation from Richmond Barracks, when he was ill, with the purpose of disrupting communi-cation between him and his legal representatives. A contemporary letter of complaint from his solicitor to the Provost Marshal of Richmond Barracks, which can be found among the papers of the Chief Secretary's Office, seems to corroborate this allegation.[51]

The text wears a series of scars, the result of Figgis's attempts to propagandise and the authorities' reaction to this. As the reviewer in the *Irish Independent* explained, 'the continuity of the narrative is interrupted at several important stages, sometimes in the middle of a sentence, and the reader is left to bridge as best he can the gaps represented by the censor's now familiar row of dots'.[52] The censor appears to have excised twenty-seven passages. Some amount to no more than a few words, while other rows of dots may represent quite lengthy cuts. From the context it is evident that a few of the offending sections referred to the general political situation, whereas others made specific reference to the conditions in particular places of incarceration. Maurice Walsh has suggested that the priority of the censor in Ireland during the revolutionary period became the curbing of 'criticism of the Irish administration itself' rather than hindering the publication of the type of nationalist propaganda that might cause general disaffection with British rule.[53] The authorities became increasingly aware of the propaganda dangers that the incarceration of political prisoners presented. Nationalist coverage of the treatment of political prisoners tended to evoke not only general resentment, but often made very specific criticisms of the policies pursued by the Irish administration in prisons. The censor's sensitivities in this regard are reflected in the consistent attention that accounts of prisoners' treatment received from the press censor,[54] so it is no surprise that *A Chronicle* drew his attention. In his preface Figgis apologises that the text is incomplete, but in truth he was probably grateful and he may even have courted the censor's intervention. The impact of the stuttering narrative is to give credibility to Figgis's complaints of arbitrary authority.

Figgis's chief device for smuggling political messages into his chronicle is both more writerly and more subtle than the strategies deployed by contemporary memoirists. Although it is Figgis's passage from freedom, through incarceration, and back to freedom that gives *A Chronicle* its narrative arc, the book is built around a series of dialogues, involving Figgis and a succession of officials that he encounters. There is the chief warder at Castlebar who Figgis represents as fissured by his nationality and his loyalty. There is a sergeant in the North Staffordshires who had signed up to defend the rights of small nations and instead found himself escorting Irish internees, describing his task as 'unpleasant' and asking 'Why every nation can't manage its own affairs without other nations butting in'. At Stafford, there is Fr Moore and the sergeant in the RAMC who describes the British policy of moderated repression, as exemplified by internment, as muddled and devised by 'grand-fatherly old fools'. Instead, he suggests, they 'should either give you a clear run, and let you make what you can of your country and take the chances; or they should wait their chance and shoot you out of hand and laugh at the racket afterwards'.[55] Figgis's opponents are not inhuman or stupid, but their humanity and intelligence are revealed through their discomfort with their role in the internment process or their acknowledgement that Figgis and his colleagues may have a valid cause.

Once encountered, Darrell Figgis is difficult to forget. *A Chronicle* is an important example of the style and mind of one of the most prolific, but least remembered, Sinn Féin propagandists of the revolutionary period. During a meditation on the dulling effects of prison Figgis reflects that if a man loses his individuality he might as well commit suicide because, for him,

> Life is meaningless unless it be for the production and perfection of
> personality; and personality is meaningless unless it be the utmost

differentiation of mind, the utmost liberty of thought and action, the utmost canvassing of desire and will, without any regard to authorities and bans and interdictions, or monstrous (literally monstrous) attempts at uniformity, imperial or otherwise.[56]

A Chronicle reflects the unique personality of its author, but it also contributes to our understanding of the collective experience of those interned in 1916.

Notes to Introduction

1 Darrell Figgis, *The House of Success* (Dublin, 1922), pp 122–3.

2 A. J. Wall, assistant secretary to the Prison Commission, to Sir Maurice Lyndham Waller, 5 July 1916, in HO144/1455/313106 (1–277) in Home Office, NA, Kew.

3 Extract from letter by Edward Bulfin in First Report by the Military Censor on the Correspondence of Irish Internees, July–Oct. 1918, in CO904/164 in Colonial Office Papers, TNA.

4 Padraic Colum, 'Darrell Figgis: A Portrait', in *Dublin Magazine*, Apr.–June 1939, p. 25. Joseph Connolly wrote that 'Figgis had a double dose of vanity and egotism and seemed eager to dominate and hold the centre in whatever company he was'. See J. Anthony Gaughan (ed.), *Memoirs of Senator Joseph Connolly (1885–1961): A Founder of Modern Ireland* (Dublin, 1996), pp 227–8.

5 Andrew E. Malone, 'Darrell Figgis', in *Dublin Magazine*, Apr.–June 1926, p. 15.

6 *Anglo-Celt*, 7 July 1917; *Anglo-Celt*, 1 Dec. 1917. This suggestion, that the leadership of Sinn Féin was comprised of individuals with 'kinks' in their personalities, was not restricted to contemporary critics. Michael Hayes later characterised many of the revolutionary activists as 'odd' or 'unusual' people. See Tom Garvin, *Preventing the Future: Why was Ireland so poor for so long?* (Dublin, 2004), pp 8–9. The Dál gCais were a powerful Munster-based dynasty during the medieval period.

7 For a full discussion of this scandal see Richard Pine, *2RN and the Origins of Irish Radio* (Dublin, 2002), pp 78–113.

8   *Weekly Irish Times*, 29 Nov. 1924; *Irish Independent*, 20 Nov. 1924.

9   The events that led to Rita North's death are murky and impossible to untangle at this remove. In a recent article on Irish abortion cases, Clíona Rattigan appears to take at face value statements given to the police following North's death. These statements suggested that North admitted attempting to self-administer an abortion, precipitating the fatal consequences. This explanation may be true but its effect was to bury with North responsibility for any crime committed, and therefore must be viewed with some suspicion. Extensive statements about the North and Figgis deaths can be found at MEPO3/2578, TNA, London. See also Clíona Rattigan, '"Crimes of passion of the worst character": Abortion cases and Gender in Ireland' in Maryann Gialanella Valiulis (ed.), *Gender and Power in Irish History* (Dublin, 2009), pp 128–9.

10   The collections of poetry were *A Vision of Life* (1909), *The Crucibles of Time and Other Poems* (1911), and *The Mount of Transfiguration* (1915). He regularly wrote literary criticism for various journals in Ireland and England and the three books which drew and expanded on this were *Shakespeare: A Study* (1911), *Studies and Appreciations* (1912) and *Æ (George Russell): A Study of a Man and a Nation* (1916). The two novels then published were *Broken Arcs* (1911) and *Jacob Elthorne: A Chronicle of Life* (1914), while Queen Tara was staged in February 1913.

11   See William Murphy, 'Darrell Figgis', in James McGuire and James Quinn (eds), *Dictionary of Irish Biography*, 3 (Cambridge, 2009), pp 775–7.

12   *Irish Independent*, 23 Feb. 1917; 15 Mar. 1917; 18 May 1917.

13   The best account of the South Longford by-election is to be found in Marie Coleman, *County Longford and the Irish Revolution* (Dublin, 2002), pp 45–67.

14   See p. 130 below.

15   *Hansard 5 (Commons)*, xciv, 1384–5, 15 June 1917.

16   *Irish Times*, 16 June 1917.

17   *Irish Independent*, 18 June 1917.

18   *Irish Times*, 7 July 1917.

19   *Irish Book Lover*, ix (1917–18), pp 80–1.

20   Darrell Figgis, *A Second Chronicle of Jails* (Dublin, 1919).

21   William Murphy, 'Narratives of Confinement: Fenians, Prisons and Writing, 1867–1916', in Fearghal McGarry and James McConnel (eds), *The Black Hand of Republicanism: Fenianism in Modern Ireland* (Dublin, 2009), pp 160–76.

22 W. J. Brennan-Whitmore, *With the Irish in Frongoch* (Dublin, 1917); Louis J. Walsh, *'On My Keeping' and In Theirs* (Dublin, 1921); Dan Breen, *My Fight for Irish Freedom* (Dublin, 1924); Tom Barry, *Guerilla Days in Ireland* (Dublin, 1949); Ernie O'Malley, *On Another Man's Wound* (London, 1936).

23 McConville refers to *A Chronicle* when describing the hardships of solitary confinement and the much better conditions experienced by those held in Reading Prison from July 1916. Seán McConville, *Irish Political Prisoners, 1848–1922: Theatres of War* (London, 2003), pp 457 and 464.

24 Robert Burnham, 'Figgis, Darrell [Edmund] (1882–1925)', in Robert Hogan (ed.), *Dictionary of Irish Literature* (London, 1996), p. 434.

25 Maryanne Wessel-Felter, 'Darrell Figgis: An Overview Of His Work', in *Journal of Irish Literature, xxii, 2* (1993), p. 5.

26 Brennan-Whitmore, *With the Irish in Frongoch*; Joseph M. Byrne, *Prisoners of War: Some Recollections of an Irish Deportee* (Dublin, 1917).

27 See p. 99 below.

28 See pp 6, 50 below.

29 Robert Hogan and Richard Burnham, *The Art of the Amateur, 1916–1920: Modern Irish Drama V* (New Jersey, 1984), p. 251.

30 See pp 33, 101, 108–9 below.

31 Anna Bryson, *The Insider: The Belfast Prison Diaries of Eamonn Boyce 1956–1962* (Dublin, 2007), pp 2–3.

32 Seán Milroy's recollections were serialised in the *Hibernian* in late 1915 and subsequently published as *Memories of Mountjoy* (Dublin, 1917), p. 45.

33 *Irish Times*, 16 June 1917; *Irish Independent*, 18 June 1917.

34 *Southern Star*, 2 Mar. 1918.

35 See p. 73 below.

36 See pp 74, 81–2 below.

37 Witness Statement of Robert Holland, WS280 in BMH, NAI.

38 See pp 51, 57, 83, 106 below.

39 See p. 116 below.

40 Malone, 'Darrell Figgis', p. 15.

41 Peadar Ó hAnnracháin, Birmingham, to Henry Dixon, 12 Aug. 1918, in MS35,262/1 (30) in Henry Dixon Papers, NLI. Figgis was known for his fastidious dress. Padraic Colum wrote that 'in a city [Dublin] where there was a good deal of carelessness in the matter of dress, Darrell Figgis was fittingly

and at the same time colourfully attired; I remember when he came to Dublin first he donned saffron kilts, and he looked mighty well in them'. Colum, 'Darrell Figgis: A Portrait', p. 22.

42   Witness Statement of Ernest Blythe, ws939 in BMH, NAI.

43   Seán T. Ó Ceallaigh, *Seán T: Scéal a bheatha á insint* (Dublin, 1963), p. 237.

44   Witness Statement of Eamonn O'Duibhir, ws1403 in BMH, NAI.

45   *A Chronicle*, p. 4.

46   See p. 78 below.

47   See pp 83–90 below. The decision to relieve the conditions that 'practically amounted to solitary confinement' was recommended by Major General Sir Wyndham Childs, the official responsible for Irish internees at the War Office, and sanctioned by General Sir John Maxwell in late May. See Sir Wyndham Childs to Sir Maurice Lyndham Waller, 3 Aug. 1916, in HO144/1455/313106 (274).

48   See pp 12, 14 below.

49   Ernie O'Malley, *Rising Out: Seán Connolly of Longford* (Dublin, 2007), p. 61.

50   See p. 21 below.

51   Edwin M. Lloyd, solicitor, to Lieutenant Colonel Fraser, Provost Marshal, Richmond Barracks, 23 May 1916, in CSORP16628/1918, NAI.

52   *Irish Independent*, 18 June 1917.

53   Maurice Walsh, *The News from Ireland: Foreign Correspondents and the Irish Revolution* (London, 2008), pp 120–1.

54   See the monthly reports of the press censor for Ireland from Aug. 1917 to Mar. 1919 in CO904/166–7 in Colonial Office Papers, TNA, London.

55   See pp 42, 94 below.

56   See p. 29 below.

Note on the text

The text of *A Chronicle of Jails* is reprinted as a facsimile of the 1917 Talbot Press edition. The original cover, dedication and prefatory note are reprinted at the start of the facsimile text, on pages xxvii, xxviii and xxix. The illustrations on page xxx have been added to this edition.

A CHRONICLE OF JAILS

DARRELL FIGGIS

¶ "Jail Journals are always a fascinating study. The self-recorded thoughts and impressions of man forcibly isolated from his fellows in the solitude of the jail have a certain interest which is hard to explain. This is the case even when the recorder is a criminal. But when, as in the present instance, the individual is a highly cultured 'political felon' making his first acquaintance with the means and methods which twentieth century civilisation has provided for the reformation of those who transgress its laws, then, indeed, we have in such a one's 'Jail Journal' something of surpassing interest."-"Mac."

DUBLIN: THE TALBOT PRESS LTD.

TO
THE LADY AT THE GATE

PREFATORY NOTE

THE following pages were written mainly as a record for myself of days in which one's private interest crossed a wider national interest, and which therefore seemed worthy of being set down with some care and faithfulness. In passing them for publication now it is necessary for me to apologise for their incompleteness in certain particulars. That incompleteness is due to no fault of mine. It has been arranged to rectify this by an edition at a subsequent date, when the contrast of edition with edition will reveal other matters relative to these days.

D. F.

"On the Run,"
    5th June, 1917

A prison mug taken as a souvenir by Figgis, 1919, EW1614. This image is reproduced with the kind permission of the National Museum of Ireland.

Millie Figgis's calling card from her period as 'The Lady at the Gate', 1916, EW5426. This image is reproduced with the kind permission of the National Museum of Ireland.

A CHRONICLE OF JAILS

By Darrell Figgis

I.

Tuesday, April 25th, 1916, was filled with sunshine, in token of the summer that was on the way, while a keen wind from the north came in reminder of the winter that was passing. The winter had been bad, and the spring but poor, so that work on the land was delayed, and there had been no fishing for the year. Yet these things had not served me ill, for I had been tied all hours with a book overdue with the publisher. For some months I had been struggling with Calendars of State Papers, in which in their introductions English editors revealed so candidly the prejudice that marked their work. So that I waited about the house during the morning, loth to begin work, and listening to the voices that came up from the land. The spring work was in full swing. Voices of men, voices of women, and the barking of dogs, flowed over the land pleasantly. Nothing seemed further removed from the day and its work than the noise of war.

Moreover, the post was late. This was another excuse for keeping from the desk. I looked along the half mile of the road till it bent behind the heath, looking for the rider on the horse that was our only connection with the big world.

It was not till some hours after noon that, looking along the road for the post that was so unaccountably late, I saw a friend making her way toward the house on her bicycle. As she came nearer and dismounted I could see the traces of tears on her cheeks, and wondered.

" The post is very late," I said.

" There is no post," she replied, " but there's terrible news. There has been fighting in Dublin. They say Dawson Street is full of dead and wounded men. The Volunteers hold the General Post Office, the Bank of Ireland, and a number of buildings all over Dublin. They've been attacking the Castle, but I cannot find out what happened there. The soldiers are attacking them everywhere with machine guns, and they say the slaughter is terrible."

The mountains stood in the sunshine, calm and splendid, with a delicate mist clothing their dark sides softly. The sea stretched out to the western horizon, its winter rage laid by, the sun glinting in the waves of the offshore wind like the spears of a countless host, and the islands of the bay, from Clare to Inish Bofin, lay in its waters like wonderful jewels that shone in the sun. Into this world of delicate beauty came this news, this tale of yet another attempt to win for a land so beautiful the freedom that other lands knew. It was not strange that the mind found some difficulty in adjusting itself to perceive a tale that came like a stream of blood across the day.

A week or so before, I had had a letter from Sheehy Skeffington telling me that the situation in Dublin was very strained. The constraint of the Censor was over the letter, and so little news was told. One knew, of course, that Dublin Castle was only looking for a chance to seize the Volunteer leaders, and one knew that the Volunteers were stiff and pledged to the utmost resistance. And Sheehy Skeffington's letter conveyed little more than that the situation was daily becoming more and more strained.

I turned for more news.

" Oh, I don't know any more," came the response. " The engine-driver of the Mail brought whatever news there is. He said that the Volunteers held most of the railway stations, and that the bridges were blown up and the tracks destroyed. Fighting was going on throughout the city when he left. That's what he says anyway, but nobody knows what to believe. It's terrible to think of. The whole country was coming round to our way of thinking, business men and responsible men everywhere were waking up with your financial agitation and other things ; and now it's all spoilt. Everything will be worse than ever now."

Already the news was spreading about the place, and knots of men were standing on the road in discussion. It was impossible to rest in the house, and so we set off through the villages to see if any further news could be learned. In one of the villages a Sunday's paper was discovered, in which appeared the General Order by Eoin MacNeill, as President and Chief of Staff of the Volunteers, countermanding manœuvres that had been ordered for Sunday—Easter Sunday. That only complicated the matter. " Owing to the very critical position "—what critical position ? What was the cause of the order ? And if " each individual Volunteer " had been ordered to refrain from " parades, marches, or other movements," how then came it about that there should be this news of fighting ? The original manœuvres, apparently, had been ordered for Sunday, whereas this news told of trouble that had broken out on Monday.

It was perplexing. The only thesis into which all the available parts seemed to fit was that it was discovered that Dublin Castle proposed to take advantage of the manœuvres on Easter Sunday to disarm the Volunteers, and, finding itself baulked by this countermanding order, had attacked headquarters and the local centres on the following day. That tallied with Sheehy Skeffington's letter, and was also all of a piece with the document which Alderman Kelly had read at a meeting of the Dublin Corporation some days previous. And that was accepted by us all as the most likely theory to account for the facts.

It was a strange day. It was a strange week.

If one's countrymen were being attacked, pretty plain and clear one's duty seemed ; but how to put it into operation ?   Over eighteen months before—after the gun-running at Howth—I had been in command of the Volunteers for the county, and at the time of the split I had sought to hold both sides together in the county.

.   .   .   .

Since then I had held to my desk.

.   .   .   .

Whereas once there had been five thousand Volunteers in the county, now two hundred exceeded their number.

.   .   .   .

The days were full of anxiety.   A few of the older people, in secure possession of their pensions, cursed the " Sinn Feiners " roundly. But most were perplexed, and told one another tales of those who in elder days had died for Ireland.   There was little else to tell.   The air was thick with rumours : rumours that were contradicted as soon as they came.   It was said that Cork and Limerick were " up," and that Kerry had seized the cable and wireless stations. This was contradicted ; and affirmed again. Wexford, it was said, was " up," and the whole county in a blaze. Hard on this followed news that Drogheda and Dundalk had risen and tried to destroy the railroads leading to the north. This last was the only exact piece of news that came from the east coast. More precise news came from Co. Galway, nearer home. The east coast news did not reach us till the Wednesday and Thursday ; but on Tuesday came news that Co. Galway was " up," and that the Volunteers there were under the command of Liam Mellowes, who had returned from exile in England, disguised as a priest, and Kenny, a famous footballer. It was stated that they had marched on the city of Galway, but had retired from there under the fire of gunboats, and had turned on Athenry, where they had encamped on one of the Department's farms. Thursday and Friday reported that this force had marched on Athlone and had destroyed the bridge there ; but that they were under retreat before a strong force of military with artillery.

This was the only piece of news that

attempted to give details. Of Dublin no
details could be learned, except that on the
Monday Lancers had charged down O'Connell
Street, but had broken in disorder under a
heavy fire and had fled, leaving many slain.
It was not till Thursday that the news of the
taking of the Bank of Ireland was contradicted ;
and at the same time it was reported that
Dublin Castle was not taken. Buildings such as
Boland's Mill, Jacob's Factory, and the Four
Courts, were said to be in possession of the
Volunteers, who were resisting desperately ;
but these names were not mentioned with
any touch of authenticity, but rather like the
names and symbols of a fantastic legend.

It was difficult to know what to believe or
know. Each succeeding day, instead of clearing
the air with more precise news, thickened the
rumours that flew, until even what finally trans-
pired to be true seemed to possess the least
likelihood of truth. The police posted reassuring
bulletins on the telegraph poles, but nobody
gave any heed to these. They were read, and
turned from in silent, deep distrust. From them
first came the news that Sir Roger Casement
had attempted to land on the coast of Kerry
with rifles from a German transport, but that he

had been arrested on landing in a small boat, and that the transport with rifles had been sunk. " German help is now at the bottom of the sea," declared the notice. Nobody believed any particle of the notice. The fact that a few of the old-age pensioners clutched the news to themselves so avidly only deepened the distrust.

From the coastguards on Wednesday news was circulated that the German Navy had attacked in force on the East Coast of England, in the attempt to effect a landing for troops ; but that all the German fleet was sunk and the English fleet had lost two battleships. One of the coastguards' wives, however, the following day was heard to state that not two, but eight battleships had been sunk on the English side ; and this spread swiftly through the villages. Little comment was made on the change in the story ; and that fact was more significant than many words.

II.

Such were the days of an anxious week. None knew what to believe, what to trust, or what to distrust. Work was impossible. Sleep even was almost impossible. We could but drift about and wait, when to do so seemed almost like a tragic cowardice. What proved finally to be well-grounded of the rumours that flew were disbelieved. What proved to be false were the only matters in which any reliance was placed. None doubted, for instance, that Cork and Limerick were " up," or that Wexford County was in a blaze, or that Ballina, quite near home, had captured Killala Bay. None placed much reliance in the rumours of fierce fighting round Boland's Mill and Jacob's Factory. None doubted that Athlone Bridge had been blown up and that the Galway boys were retreating from the town, contesting every foot of the way against a large English force. None believed in the landing and capture of Casement.

One of the county papers published a special edition on Thursday recording all the rumours. " The Mayo News," however, refused in its edition on the Saturday to print or give ordinary circulation to any rumours, and advised its readers to wait patiently until some reliable news was to hand. The question of food had become a matter of alarm, for now that the Rising had lasted a week, it might well last much longer, with strange results to follow. And a good part of one's efforts were occupied with discovering where flour was available.

Then on the Monday came news that Padraic Pearse had surrendered, and that the Commandants under him were accepting the order, though reluctantly. The first week's strain was released, but the mood of the people began to make a slow change, such a change as Pearse had foreseen. Already in the first week that change has appeared; but the news now told of defeat, an ancient tale in Ireland, full of old honour. On Tuesday the mail was resumed. Papers came and were passed eagerly from hand to hand. The people were afraid, but sullen. Martial law gave unlimited power to the peelers, who continued in bands of three and four with carbines slung over their shoulders along the roads ; but the Rising was already beginning to take its place among Ireland's tragic efforts for freedom. The causes were not known ; men had, in fact, ceased to wonder whether it had been a planned Rising or a provoked resistance. The outstanding fact was its utter failure ; and that became its greatest success, for so it became kneaded into a history never very far from an Irishman's emotional consciousness. And when the further news came that a large part of the city of Dublin was in ruins as the effect of artillery fire, and when steadily through the week the tale came of execution succeeding to execution, the sullenness changed to exasperation. Even those who during the Rising had been whole-hearted in their denunciation of it, became bitter of speech.

Not the least cause inducing this were the wholesale arrests that were being reported from all over the country. I had already been warned, many months previously, that my arrest had been determined for the very first chance I gave certain persons at Dublin Castle. The warning had come through a friendly channel, and I had accepted it as a compliment to my intrusions in public affairs. But now the case was different, for one's political opponents were clothed with unlimited power. Moreover, there was another thing that gave me reason to fear.

.   .   .   .

Yet when that week was passed, and the greater part of the next, I began to think that my schedule would never be called, in spite of the fact that each day's paper recorded a general sweep-up all through the country. On May 10, I went to bed late as usual. I had been setting potatoes all day, and had been working making a precis of State Papers till late at night. I retired at about two o'clock in the morning. As I turned into bed, a strong presentiment came on me suddenly, almost like an oppression, that I was to be arrested the following morning. It was so strong that I thought to wake my wife ; but, feeling ashamed of it, I lay wakeful and wondering.

III.

Two hours later I was wakened by the heavy tread of many feet down the road. A large number of men were passing round the house. We leapt out of bed, and, peering through the windows, could see two peelers at each window, with rifles at the " ready."

A man who was down on the foreshore, with my house between him and the village, afterwards described the scene. The whole force of eighteen peelers, three sergeants, and a district inspector, had charged down my *boithrin* at the double—charged down on a house in which one man, one woman, eight hens and fifteen chickens lay asleep. There was little need for so desperate an attack.

.   .   .   .   ‘   .   .

Agitated counsels could point no better way than a peaceful surrender ; so I went out to

the porch, and through the window spoke to
the district inspector. I told him that my wife
was dressing, and that I would stand there in
his sight if he would give her a few moments
in which to put a few clothes about her before
his men took possession of the house. He
agreed. But the local sergeant had other notions
of the proper and fitting thing to be done on so
auspicious an occasion. Some baulks of timber
were lying about the house, and with these, and
some heavy rocks, he set about to batter down
the doors.

.   .   .   .

Two peelers came into the bedroom with me
while I dressed, while the others tied every
available piece of paper that could be found into
parcels. And after a hurried breakfast I was
borne off on a motor car for Castlebar Jail, with
a peeler sitting each side of me, and one in front,
beside the driver, with loaded carbines. It
was a cold, miserable morning, and a hurricane
of wind and rain swept about the car.

IV.

Castlebar was my first jail. I was more fortunate than many who were swept-up during those days. I was at least accorded a prison-cell.

.   .   .   .

Compared with these things, which I learned afterwards, my condition was kingly. I was treated as an ordinary criminal.

The events of the day had presumably come with too great a shock to make much effect, for I was all the time strangely unperturbed and calm. It was only when all my things had been taken from me and I was placed in a reception-cell that the reaction came. A reception-cell is about two-thirds the size of an ordinary cell, with only a small window, and very dark. Its only furniture is a little stool. When the door clanged against me and the key grated in the lock, an almost overpowering desire came on me to shout aloud and batter on the door with my fists. That was succeeded by a feeling of utter helplessness. Tears had need to be controlled. I remember resolving never to permit the caging of a bird, although that had always been a principle with me. For now the principle took a new and poignant shape.

I was left there an hour or so (time ceased to count when emotion became so much more heavily charged) before being removed to my allotted cell. Castlebar Jail is constructed like the letter V. The building runs down each side of the V, with a high wall connecting the base, thus making a triangle of the whole. Each wing contains one line of cells, on each of the two floors, in the outer wall. The space included in the triangle is open to the sky, is floored with flints (up through which two daisies nevertheless grew), and is used as a special exercise yard. The main large yard lies beyond the left wing. Two distinctive features of Castlebar Jail stand out in my memory as contrasted with the English jails I was to visit. The English jails were built of red brick, warm to the eye. Castlebar Jail was built of grey granite, cold and forbidding, like a dungeon. On the other hand, the cells and passages of the English jails were floored with stone, whereas Castlebar Jail was

floored with timber. I was to appreciate the
virtue of this later. One other difference is
worthy of note. All the English jails were of
considerable size. Castlebar Jail is quite small.
The difference is noteworthy because it signified
a difference in the number of criminals expected,
and in fact, as I learnt while there, Castlebar
Jail had been specially re-opened because of the
Rising-Out.

The reception cell in which I had been placed
lay on the ground floor of the right-hand wing,
near the entrance at the apex. My appointed
cell was on the first floor of the left-hand wing,
near the base. There I saw for the first time,
what was later to become a familiar sight in
other places—the equipment of a cell. In the
far left-hand corner stood the bed-board, raised
on end against the wall, with blankets draped
over it. At its base was coiled the mattress.
In the middle of the right-hand wall stood the
little table, with a stool beside it ; and on the
wall hung a copy of the prison rules.

A cheerless morning, a cheerless experience,
and a cheerless abode. Even grimness, that
faithful consolation in adversity, was hard to
summon. I put down my bed-board and
stretched the mattress upon it, wishing to forget

everything in sleep. But in a short while the warder passing on his round looked through the spyhole in the door. The key grated in the lock, and I was roughly told to put up the board at once and to arrange the things as I had found them. No bed-board was allowed to remain down after five o'clock in the morning or to be put down before half past eight at night.

The warder was a dark-visaged man, with a harsh northern accent. He shouted when he spoke as though he addressed a herd of cattle. He was a fair specimen on the warder side of an inhuman system, and one could imagine from his manner the men whom he was accustomed to handle. One could imagine, too, the soulless beings prisoners must inevitably become under such a man and with such surroundings. Either they must become meek and cringing, or, in the effort to defy so abject a fate, they must become turbulent and violent. The former meant a life of peace ; the latter meant a life of ceaseless torture ; but the latter was at any rate a more honourable estate. After shouting threats and abuse at me with which the whole prison resounded—after informing me that he would soon dress me into shape, grand and all as I was—

the warder went out, leaving me feeling as though I had been pitched into a cesspool.

Yet his visit was salutary. It whipped one out of one's misery, and gave one something to fight for. I turned to the rules on the wall and read them carefully and completely. The jail having been newly re-opened, the Governor was a Chief Warder acting as Governor. (This I afterwards perceived, for I did not then know the distinction between Chief Warders and Governors.) Later in the morning he entered to give me my instructions for the day; and when he did so, I had sufficiently mastered the section relating to " Prisoners Awaiting Trial " to interrogate him on its application to myself. I claimed the right to books, to tobacco, to daily newspapers, to daily letters out and in, to daily visitors, to my own meals ordered from the town, and to getting another prisoner, if I so wished it, to clean out my cell each day.

Whatever was there to be claimed, I claimed. At first he sought to put me by. But when I compelled him to an admission that I was at least a " Prisoner Awaiting Trial " then I claimed the fulfilment of the rights accorded to that type of prisoner. It required some address at first to get him to converse, for the usual method was harshly and instantly to strike down any attempt at conversation. It was necessary at first, quite casually and calmly, to ask an interpretation of the rules ; and then, once the net of discussion was cast, it was not so difficult to hold him in its toils.

He looked at me as though he wished he had removed the troublesome rules. " You forget," he said, " these aren't ordinary times. You are under martial law now. The soldiers are the masters of us all now, so they are. I amn't very sure that I know where I am myself. Rules don't apply now. Nothing applies. I get my instructions from day to day. They might take you out to-morrow morning and shoot you, so they might, and nobody to save you. Isn't the whole of the City of Dublin in ruins ? I cannot give you but what I'm bid, and those rules don't relate to you—they don't relate to anybody."

He granted me permission, however, to send out for my meals, if I so wished it, and to write one letter each day, on a sheet provided for that purpose. As a tally against the failure of my other rights he agreed that I might keep my bed-board down for certain hours of the day :

a concession that very much perplexed my northern warder.

I learnt from the other prisoners afterwards that this Governor was very rough and harsh with them. At first he was so with me ; but finally he shewed me as much kindliness as was possible under the circumstances. He did so in a strange way. He would enter my cell and shout at me as harshly as at any ; and then he would close the door, sit on my stool, and begin to talk quite humanly. Such conversations would conclude as brusquely and sharply as they began. Thus a certain kinship emerged between us. We were both Irishmen, with a stranger's martial hand against us both, thrusting me into jail, and abrogating his rules. In that mood he always spoke to me as one fellow-countryman might to another of some unintelligible foreigner that had come into our land ; and then he would remember that he was leagued with the foreigner, whereas I was pledged against him, when he would make some curt remark and leave me.

V.

Later in the morning I heard the jingle of the warder's keys, the grating of locks, and the tramp of feet down the wooden passage outside. Presently it came to my turn, and my door was flung open. When I made no move, my warder appeared in the doorway with angry countenance to ask me what I was doing.

" Am I wanted ? " I asked.

" You're to come out to exercise, and look sharp. If you've a coat there, bring it with you, it's raining."

Through the small high window, ribbed with heavy bars and paned with thick, dirty glass, it was impossible to say what sort of a day passed by outside. The different texture of the twilight within was the only indication.

I was taken to the big yard, and there, for the first time, I saw my fellow-prisoners. There was an Excise Officer, two men whom I did not know, and two Gaelic League organisers. One of these last, as I entered the yard, threw up his hand in a Connacht salute, and greeted me : "Sé ᴅo ḃeaṫa, a ḋuine cóiṟ." It was surely a strange welcome to a prison yard ; and the warder's voice barked out across the yard : " Stop that talking there." I was instructed to keep my distance from the others behind and before, and in silence we all walked round and round the yard under a cold drizzling rain.

Afterwards I learnt that a large batch of Westport men had been sent to Dublin two days before, and that the prison was now beginning to fill up again. This, apparently, was the reason of the delay in my arrest. The police could only arrest as the prisons gave them space.

.   .   .   .

For Ireland's prisons were not able to keep pace with this new (and yet not so very new) manufacture of criminals.

For an hour we marched round in silence ; and then we were taken in for our dinners. The two Gaelic League organisers had been appointed as the prison orderlies. Warders never do any work, that being an offence to the relative height at which they are placed ; all work is done by prisoners under their direction. Therefore, Sean Seoighe brought me in my dinner ; and when I in my ignorance asked for a knife and spoon with which to eat it, he, on his week-old experience of jails, passed quickly out into the passage to control his mirth, leaving me to the astonishment of the warder, who asked me if I knew where I was. The astonishing nature of my request seemed to rob the warder of his asperity, for he went out in silence, leaving me to an old horn prison spoon.

At three o'clock we were taken out again for exercise, and by that time I had already fallen into prison craft. Old criminals, I was told, develop it to such an extent that their communications with one another, in the friendships they establish, become almost as complete as in ordinary life, despite the close scrutiny under which they are kept at all times. I can well understand it ; for here were we, new to the game, and without any experienced hand among us, bringing all our wits to work in order to establish communication with one another— that communication between man and man without which life is as unhealthy as a standing pool. Our minds became cunning and crafty ; the whole being became watchful and alert for

opportunities that had to be caught swiftly
as they passed, while the outward manner maintained a deceptive innocence. The result was
not conscious ; or at least it was only half-
conscious ; for a new kind of reflex seemed to
be developed. As we walked round the yard,
for instance, we timed our journey with the
warder, who walked up and down a small path
by the prison wall. The result was that we were
walking toward the far end of the yard as he
walked away from us toward the prison door.
Thus his back would be turned just as we
reached the most favourable part of our round,
and by that time the distances between us
would have become reduced as though quite
naturally. It was a manœuvre that, ordinarily,
would have been difficult to execute, yet it was
managed quite simply, and, as it were, naturally.
Then, as we passed round the favourable bend—
while the warder was walking away from us
down his little path—a swift conversation would
proceed, in voices pitched just to reach the man
before or the man behind, and without any
perceptible movement of the lips. And by the
time the warder had turned about we were
slowly finishing the bend with lengthening
distances between us, erect, and with calm

faces forward. Thus we came to know who we all were, where we were taken, the circumstances that attended our arrests, and soforth. This play of wit became no small part of the daily life ; and the penalties that were involved gave spice to existence.

When we were taken back to our cells I had a fairly exact knowledge of who my fellow-prisoners were, and who had been there before me, and when they had been removed. One became part of a new continuity, and I had a strange feeling as though I had been in prison for a long time. Supper was taken at five, and consisted of prison cocoa and bread. It was the last meal for the day, and the only thing left to do was to wait for darkness. In Castlebar Jail the gas jet projects an inch into the cell, and is never lit except during the winter months. For though prisons are sometimes spoken of as reformatories of character, yet elaborate precautions are taken to prevent suicide. Hence the horn spoons. Hence also the rope or wire netting beneath the landings. Hence the gas jet, for from anything in the nature of a bracket a man might hang himself. And such precautions are very necessary. As I sat in my cell waiting for darkness to come, I felt for the first time the beginnings of the system on me. The blank, bare walls, the high, dark window, the deathly silence outside, broken only by the occasional tread of the warder, the jingle of his keys by his side, and the sound of the cover of the spy-hole as he slid it aside to spy in upon me—all these outward things joined, with the instant repression of every sign of humanity, by communication with a fellow-prisoner, or by a word with the warder, to produce a mental blank and a complete absence of any part of the rhythm or colour of life. One never sees anything resembling a smile on warders' faces : they seem tutored to graveness or sullenness, as though they wore masks, and the only human exchange one can sometimes catch is through the eyes—a quick flash there will sometimes let one know that this warder at least is still a man and has yet not wholly become a machine. So one never sees flowers in prison (save for one exception that I was to meet, where the exception was rooted in literary history) ; and prison yards are always floored with shards of flint or coal slack, or something very like ashes. Colours are never seen, and I remember later with what extraordinary joy I feasted my eyes on a blanket with which I was provided—crimson, and yellow, and claret—a wonderful thing. Everything is toneless, colourless, featureless, expressionless, noiseless (unless the noise be the harsh voice of a warder) void and unhuman.

In the twilight that thickened in my cell I sat that first night feeling these influences sink into my soul—or rather, I felt them advancing toward me, with intent to blot out the thing that was I, the personality that was my being, without which I was not. And I was afraid, afraid as of some last obscenity. I have read those who have recommended meditation before such a grey void, so to purchase the final liquidation into the great everlastingly-flowing Nirvana. To such, a prison can be commended. Such a philosophy has never commended itself to me, to whom Life is meaningless unless it be for the production and perfection of personality ; and personality is meaningless unless it be the utmost differentiation of mind, the utmost liberty of thought and action, the utmost canvassing of desire and will, without any regard to authorities and bans and interdictions, or monstrous (literally monstrous) attempts at uniformity, imperial or otherwise. And so I sat there on my stool beside my little table, feeling the first pressure of a cold enormity muffling Life at every turn, seeking to reduce me to the utter blankness that is its ideal. The prison system protects itself by a number of contrivances against the suicide of its victims ; but suicide is indeed the logical outcome of the system, it is its final perfection.   When personality has been so far repressed that it can make no demonstration of itself, neither by voice nor signal ; when personality looks upon faces that are as expressionless as the white-washed wall and flint-strewn yard ; when the mind at last echoes the blankness it meets with a blankness as fitting, and the outer world becomes forgotten, literally forgotten :—what difference is there between such a state and the final quenching of the spark of life in a body whose only value is that a soul inhabits it ?   The last state is simply a logical completion of the first.

Thought ?   I had during my life conceived of prison as a place where a man could in silence and solitude think out things.   As I sat in my cell that first night in prison I knew on a sure insight (what I was later to prove) that this was all wrong.   As though something spake, it in my soul, I knew that thought would become sluggish and slow, and finally would not exist at all, until even the effort to recall the names and faces of friends would be relinquished as too fatiguing. I knew that ; I divined it that first night instantly ; and I was afraid. Some of the others told me that they wept every night ; and I understood it. But when the darkness compelled me to make up my bed, I simply took off my coat and collar and boots, and rolled the blankets about me as I lay down, determined that I was going to make a fight for it.

The following morning, when the Chief Warder came to see me, I started again on the rules and regulations. We fought long and hard ; and finally he granted me permission to get a daily paper and to smoke one pipe a day. " Only," he said, " you must smoke it outside, and you must smoke it in a special yard by yourself where the smell of the tobacco won't annoy the others." I agreed ; and before he left me he took the " Rules " from the wall and bore them away with him.

So I took my exercise that morning by myself, in the small yard between the forks of the prison building. My pipe was presented to me, and my pouch. When the pipe was filled, I was presented with a match, and I was watched while I lit up. Then my pouch was taken away and the door was locked behind me and I was left alone.

The yard was very small, and triangular. It had apparently not been much used, for the flints lay loose upon the surface of the ground, save for one little circle in the centre that had been trodden hard. Two sides of the triangle were formed by the prison, the walls of which rose sheer above me, cold and grey, with menacing barred windows at regular intervals. On the third side a high wall of masonry made the base of the triangle. The day was sunlit, but the sunlight could only fall across a small corner of the yard. Two daisies were growing in the centre of the circle : which I picked, and instantly regretted the selfishness and vandalism of the deed.

I walked round and round, smoking my pipe ; but when my pipe was finished, the folly of my decision faced me. Here I was shut for another hour on a floor of flints, surrounded by oppressive grey walls that rose sheer above me, with nothing to look upon but walls and floor, and high above me a patch of blue sky, across which clouds sailed. Deeply I envied the other men their sight of one another, and their craft and tricks to outwit the warder. I walked round and round the little circle, first one way and then the other ; and gave that up. I tried lying down in the corner, where the sunlight fell ; but found flint shards not the most inviting of seats. And it seemed an interminable time before the warder unlocked the door to unloose me from what had become a refined form of torture.

Yet I did not admit defeat. As I came away, the Chief Warder offered me another pipe in the afternoon, on the same terms ; and I accepted. But that was enough. The prison cell was better than that little yard, flint-strewn, beneath grey walls and barred windows. When I came back in the afternoon I took occasion to slip up the flap from the spy-hole, unobserved ; and the warder closed the door without noticing this. So I was enabled to relieve the tedium of my cell by looking out. Opposite my spy-hole was a window looking down into the yard that I had left ; and there, to my astonishment, I saw a hat passing round and round, coming into sight, and passing out of sight. The hat just appeared over a bar of the window, which hid the face of the wearer. A hat, and no more ; like a tantalising glimpse into another world ; but something about that

D

hat struck me as familiar. It was astonishingly like the hat of P. J. D., the editor and proprietor of " The Mayo News," the one paper that had refused to print any rumours during the week of the Rising. Had he then joined me in jail ?

That night when at supper I asked for the daily letter I had been promised, the Chief Warder informed me that he had received instructions from the military authorities that I was not to be permitted any sort of communication with the outer world, by letter or by visit. The previous day I had written to my wife saying that my daily letters were to be a sign to her that I was safe and well, and would show her where I was. I wish no man the hours I spent that night.

VI.

The next morning I asked the Chief Warder if he had any labour gang at which I could be employed, for I dreaded a continuance of the thoughts that had been with me through the night.

" I can put you moulding my potatoes," he said, with the air of a man who spoke of something so ridiculous that it disposed of itself.

" Very well," I said.

" Can you mould potatoes ? " he said.

He seemed to be diffident now when his humour took actual shape.

" I can try," I said. " I was eight hours setting them the day before you took me."

So a Gaelic League organiser, an Excise man,

.   .   .   .

were employed throughout that day moulding the Chief Warder's potatoes ; we enjoyed the work ; and we enjoyed it none the less because of the new warder under whom we were placed. This warder had made his first appearance, as far as I was concerned, the previous day. The mask he wore was not sour, but melancholy; and that in itself was a great difference. His voice, too, suggested possibilities. It was southern, and somewhere muffled in its official brevity a human quality echoed. I had heard that quality instantly when, the previous day, he came into my cell to bid me hasten as he had others to attend to besides myself. I had not hastened; but, quite deliberately, I had stood and looked at him. " 'Tis queer criminals you have these times, warder," I said. I looked at him; and he looked at me. Then he went to the door, looked up and down the passage, and returned to me. " Faith, you're right, sir," he said. " 'Tis a queer sort of criminals these times." It would be hard to express all that he managed to convey in those few words. Perhaps the melancholy mask he wore was all the more melancholy because of the thoughts he could not utter. Strange pass for a man when his hand is bought against his fellow-country-men; and strangest of all when his heart is not bought with his hand. We had no cause to regret our warder during that day's labour;

but I am sure he was not as sorry for us as I was for him.

He was with us on Sunday also. It being Sunday, we only received one hour's exercise during the morning; and as the Chief Warder and his other officials had gone to Mass the warder was in sole charge of us. Therefore we all had exercise together; and when I entered the yard I saw that my guess of Friday was correct, for there was P. J. D. already before me. He threw up his hand in welcome, and a smile lit over his face. I passed over and walked behind him.

There were many new faces there. There were about sixteen or seventeen of us. Some were in prison clothes.

.   .   .   .

Some had come into conflict with English troops with whom they had been stationed.

I turned to note the others in civilian clothes. One was an elderly man, with grey beard and majesterial manner: I never found out who he was. The man, however, who struck me most walked just ahead of P. J. D. Tall and athletic of build, he strode round and round the path, the very embodiment of wrath. His face, when I caught a side glance of it as he turned each bend, was black and lowering. Once as we came round the corner that served so well for our quick interchanges, he turned about, took a quick glance at the warder's retreating back, and shook his fist at the prison and all it signified, and said : " By God, but there'll be a big judgment to pay for all this yet." Then he strode on again, striking his heels on the ground. He had probably just completed his first night in jail ; and his emotion had not yet become transmuted into something more settled and grim. " Keep your heart up, man, keep your heart up," I heard P. J. D. whisper. " There's plenty of time before all of us."

VII.

When I was wakened the following morning I was informed that I had to be ready for removal in an hour's time. The Chief Warder did not know where I was to go, only that at six a guard of soldiers would come for me. It was his opinion that I was to be taken for the courtsmartial in Dublin. That meant anything; it meant, to be more precise, whatever the police desired or intended, for the reign of terror was abroad in the land, and every man's fate was decreed by whatever the police had decided would make an appropriate chapter in his *leabhran* at Dublin Castle, without other evidence than the evidence of the compilers. During those days that man was safest who was permitted to remain in any one place for a length of time, for presumably the present orgy of blood and long sentences, of courtsmartial, and authority on its war-steed champing the ground, would begin to pall. Nevertheless, I welcomed the change. Anything seemed better than inaction. It was better to go out and take one's fate thar to stay skulking in a cell. My only anxiety was for my wife, who would know nothing of my removal, and from whom it seemed decided to withhold all knowledge of me.

P. J. D. came down after me to the office where our " effects " were handed back to us. We were to be fellow travellers on the road, and we were marched through the streets of Castlebar to the Railway Station under a sergeant's guard of eight men. It was too early for the town to be astir, and those who were abroad seemed rather abashed by the spectacle. At the station, as the train came in, to my great joy I was hailed by my wife, who, not getting the promised daily letter, had travelled down by the same train that was to take me to Dublin to discover what was happening. A little tactful authority with the sergeant included her in the same carriage with ourselves ; and thus began a co-operation, from without and from within jail, that was to be of rare value in the future.

Again I was fortunate in my custodian. The sergeant belonged to one of the North Staffordshire battalions that had been rushed over for the Rising-Out, and he was a kindly, homely man, very much unlike some of his guard. The songs that came from the adjoining compartment were clearly meant to hearten us with the thought of friendship. There was no timidity in the choice of theme, and the peeler who accompanied us (as guide to the strangers in charge of his own countrymen) was clearly restive hearing songs it had become his first instinct to baton. But the sergeant was in command, and he maintained a strict dignity. At Athlone our companions next door managed to convey the state of affairs to others on the platform, with the result that the cheering crowd had time to vent their feelings outside our door before they were swept away. Then a peeler on the platform beckoned to our sergeant, and whispered something to him. When he returned to his seat beside me, I asked him what had been said to him.

" He was telling me to be careful, as there are sympathisers of yours in the next compartment and on the platforms."

" That doesn't surprise you, sergeant, does it ? " I asked.

He thought for a moment ; then, " No, sir,

it doesn't," he said. And after a minute's further thought, he added : " It's easy for me to see who has the people's wish, and who has the unpleasant job. You mustn't think, sir, I like it ; for I don't. It wasn't for this kind of thing I joined up. Why every nation can't manage its own affairs without other nations butting in, I can't for the life of me imagine. I thought it was to stop that kind of thing they told me I was wanted out in Belgium."

Apparently he had been driven to thought. He was a tall, strongly-built man, with a long head and grave face—the kind of man who takes life very seriously and very earnestly. He came from the pottery district, where he had been employed in some clerical capacity ; and when he told me he was fond of books I knew at once what kind of company he kept and what kind of books he read. In that company the cause of small nationalities had given him much heart-searching. Very earnestly he had thought the thing out, and in an international morality not at all lightly gotten-by, he had donned khaki, won his stripes, and been dispatched to Ireland for first service. I have wondered sometimes how he got on in Belgium. Perhaps he laid down his life in order that small nations should have freedom declared as their indefeasible right.

At Dublin, when I suggested that P. J. D. and I should hire cars across to Richmond Barracks, and that he should divide his guard between us, he willingly accepted the proposal.

VII.

At Castlebar rigorous care was taken that P. J. D. and I should not speak with one another. Care had been taken that we should exercise apart, and only by the accident of the shortage of staff on the Sunday had either of us been able to do more than guess at the other's presence. At Richmond Barracks we were thrown together perforce, and were condemned to sleep under the one slender blanket.

In the room to which we were consigned there were already twenty-five others. The officers who took us up told me that it was known as the Leaders' Room : a description that, at that time, was . . . ominous . . . . From it, De Valera had gone to his life's sentence ; from it, I was told, Sean MacDiarmada had gone to his death . . . . ; and there Count Plunkett had been required to answer for the consciences of his sons. And a goodly company remained there yet, from

whom we received a hospitality the joviality
of which gave no heed to the courtsmartial that
slowly worked their way along the lists provided
by a diligent officialdom. Presents from
friends were permitted, under supervision ; and
food so obtained was put into a common com-
missariat, presided over by mighty Sean
O'Mahony, the ruler and president of our company. From this store we were regaled without
further ado, while he stood between us and the
others who rose to welcome us to our fate. He
would suffer none to approach us with a more
immediate welcome or inquiry until we had had
what we would of the hospitality it was his to
dispense ; and then we mixed in the company
into which we had been cast.

So, for the first time I came into touch with
those who had had their part in the Rising.
There were some of the company on whom the
burning yet remained. Most had been through
a historic week, and three had been severely
wounded. In all cases these were leg wounds
from bullets, and two of the number had been
lying on the wooden floor, covered by blankets,
when we entered. Coming as I did from a part
of the country where only wild, whirling rumours
had reached, sound and fury of things that had

and things that had not occurred, there was something of a thrill in this first touch of the actual event. One faded into insignificance beside the simplest follower that had borne the heat of the day. He would be a man of little emotion, surely, who did not feel as I did at that moment, with a touch of awe and respect kindling in his veins. It seemed then to me a little thing that a man should think and .labour for his country beside those who had offered dear life for her sake.

Therefore, when one of the wounded men limped up to me, claiming an acquaintance I had forgotten, I was anxious to discover from him where he had fought, and to learn some details of the fighting. He had, with high personal courage and ability, filled one of the commands in the defence of the South Dublin Union, and was not loth to tell his tale. But our conversation was overheard, and an uproar rose.

" He's going to tell about the South Dublin Union again. No, no ; that can't be allowed. We're tired about the South Dublin Union." I protested that I wished to hear. " I'm sorry, but we can't permit it. We've heard that story so often that it's not safe for us to hear it again. It's really not safe. If you let him, he'll tell it you for a week ; but we can't permit it ; we've our nerves to consider."

So it was. In no way could I extract my tale, and had to remain without it.

.   .   .   .

IX.

Richmond Barracks was for the military the clearing house for rebels ; for the police it was their last chance of a stroke.

.   .   .   .

Marching tunes are in military orders, and the men in khaki perceived no difference between one tune and another ; but the little groups in dark green became twice as sullen, and twice as anxious to lay their victims by the heels, one way or another. Without a doubt Richmond Barracks was of great value from the dramatic point of view.

We were housed in the second and third storey rooms of the barracks. The troops occupied the ground floor, the guards were posted at the doors and on the landings,

while outside the whole building was enclosed
with barbed wire barricades, guarded again
by soldiers. It was to Richmond Barracks
that the men of the Republican Army were swept
as they surrendered. Some were taken to
Kilmainham and Arbour Hill, the Castle and
other places.

.   .   .   .

Not till Asquith's visit were these things
rectified ; and even thereafter conditions were
only slowly, and, as it were, grudgingly,
amended. By the time I arrived at the clearing-
house, a fortnight after the Rising had concluded,
the amendment was in progress.

The cause for this was simple. Far more
potent than a very questionable beneficence
in Premiers, was the grim and bitter mood that
had settled on the country. This had to be
propitiated. Asquith's visit was but a token
of political sagacity ; and while I was at Richmond, the dawning of the same sagacity on the

E

military mind could be seen in the shape of extra blankets, extra and better food, benches to sit on, tables to eat from, knives, spoons and forks to eat with, and some care for greater cleanliness. Slowly these things came ; not exactly with a remarkable good humour or good will ; and were received by us, as they came one by one, with ribaldry and laughter.

Thus, soon after our arrival P. J. D. and I were apportioned a blanket apiece, and at night-fall, on the call of the bugle, we were instructed by the others in their use. We all slept with our heads to the wall and our feet toward the centre of the room. We slept in couples for the better use of our blankets. One blanket was stretched on the floor, the other served for coverlet, and our coats made our pillows. So we slept each night, fully dressed, for the nights were bitterly cold. It was extraordinary how soon one's hip-bones hardened to the floor, and the simplicity of toilet was a great boon to anyone who had found dressing and undressing labyrinths of inconvenience.

In the morning the reveille sounded at six o'clock ; and from then until about eight we were taken out in squads under armed guards, to wash at the pumps and washbowls in the yard.

For our meals, we sat where we could or would, on the ground, or, if one were tactful, on the window-sills. We were all allowed to retain up to a pound in cash, and some of the men had purchased jack-knives from the soldiers. Others had managed to retain their own pen-knives. Such men were fortunate, for they were able at once to proceed with their meals. The others either waited until an implement was available, or they did not wait.

Yet all these were but campaigning inconveniences. The great thing was that we were, by necessity, permitted one another's company ; and the utmost joviality prevailed. None would have thought that in one of the barrack buildings within sight of our windows, the courtsmartial were sitting, and that men were being picked out from the rooms and sent to long terms of penal servitude. No one knew whose turn would come next. The selections were, by any reckoning, an extraordinary hazard. Some who confidently expected a summons, were passed over in silence. Others were selected whose choice was inexplicable, except on the supposition (which indeed was no supposition) that some local spite was exerted against them. Any evening an officer might enter and hand a man a paper form. That form was a state-ment of the case against him, and meant that on the following day he was to be taken before the Court Martial. No time was given to prepare a defence or employ counsel. The next morning he was taken out. If his case were not heard, he returned that evening, and would go forth in the morning ; if his case were heard, he would not return, and we would know nothing until, in the course of a week or ten days, his sentence was promulgated in the papers.

One such case stands out vividly in my memory because of an interesting personal relation that was suggested. Thrice a certain officer had entered, and we had all stood in a line before him while he, accompanied by a detective, inspected us each carefully in turn. Each time he had turned away dissatisfied ; and on the third occasion, as he did so, one of our number made some jest, at which we all laughed. Instantly the officer turned about and fixed on one of our number.

" You're Captain L——, aren't you ? " he said.

" I am."

" You were at the Post Office, in charge of the prisoners ? "

" I was."

" Just so.   I didn't recognise you out of your uniform.   You are the man.   I fixed you just now when you laughed by your gold teeth."

When he had gone we gathered round L—— to ask him who the man was ; and we learned that he had been a prisoner in the Post Office. When the Post Office had been set on fire, and became untenable, the building had been evacuated in haste.   Not until they were filing out into the street were the prisoners remembered, and then O'Rahilly had sent L—— back to bring them out to safety.   As the prisoners were housed in a room next to that in which the ammunition and high explosives were stored, beside the lift-shaft, down through which the sparks were falling, this was a task of some considerable danger.

.   .   .   .

X.

Men so selected went off to a criminal's fate.
Yet the authorities in effect recognised that the
selection turned on a hazard by treating us all
as criminals. Forms were delivered on some
men with charges that astonished none so much
as the recipients ; and as there was no evidence
other than police reports offered in support of
such allegations, the only thing in doubt was
the length of the sentence. On the other hand,
men were passed over who were not less astonished at the passing. But all our finger-prints
were taken. We were afterwards considerably
amused at the assurance given in the English
House of Commons that finger-prints were only
taken " at first " " owing to the difficulty of
identification," and that they were taken
"under military supervision." Finger-prints were
taken all the time I was at Richmond Barracks
by a peeler whose descent on newcomers was
greeted with ironic mirth, for he was a familiar

figure as he hung about the barracks like a hawk, carrying his implements with him. What mirth we had we made as we went, for all that it had a grim background ; but we were certainly assisted by comparing the declarations in Parliament as to our estate with the conditions we actually endured. And the idea of any " difficulty of identification " was a joke more than ordinarily grim. It conveyed a wonderful conception of Ireland as a land untracked and uncharted ; whereas, in the most elaborately policed country in the world the only thing lacking to make our *leabhrain* artistically complete was the presence of a finger-print. And the artists in dark green were swift to complete their pictures.

Such things, I found, were only treated with mirth. It was curious to note the way in which the doings of the police—either of the R.I.C. or the D.M.P., " two minds with but a single aim, two hearts that beat as one "— were received. There was a bitterness in the ribaldry with which they were greeted, a bitterness and a certain frosty sting in the mirth ; but there was also the laughter for relief.

.   .   .   .

Not having been in Richmond Barracks during the first days of terror, I raised a complaint the following morning with the medical officer. I asked his co-operation, as an Irishman who should resent a national insult. He did resent it ; and as a result, the young officer was compelled to apologise as a matter of discipline. Thereafter, that officer appeared no more among us ; but neither did the medical officer.

Yet, in spite of all these things, we had one another ; and that was compensation. I had heard of most of my companions before, but had never had the opportunity of meeting many of them ; and I was now glad of the chance of acquaintance and discussion. In Richmond the first beginnings appeared of that cementing of brotherhood among the " prisoners of war " that was afterwards to take so fine a form. About a fortnight after my arrival some of us in our room were offered special rooms, with two beds in each room ; but we all refused these without any further enquiry rather than injure or forego that brotherhood. Our national convictions were the same in fundamentals, but they took different forms. Our roots were the same, and they were set in the same good earth ; but the branches and blossoms were various. From afar, we could only see the branches and blossoms, and were chiefly aware of our differences from one another ; but now that we came near one another we could see that our roots were in the same soil.

Indeed, some came who had few roots to boast of, but roots were soon generated, partly by the warmth of suitable companionship, partly by the heat engendered by their treatment. And with all, save a possible few exceptions, a unity and kinship was soon evolved, that mitigated the hardship of our estate and wiped away the sense of danger that hung over us all.

Our comradeship softened our hardship in other ways also. The English Army was camped round about us to stop all communication with the outer world except through the permitted channels. We were allowed two visits a week. Our visitors stood on one side of the barbed wire and we stood on the other, with an armed guard between us. All parcels and letters had to pass through the censor. If the parcels contained clothing, we received them ; if they contained food, we did not receive them. That was a part of the rapacity of the army we did not appreciate ; but there was another side to it. We were encompassed

about with traders, and so, by uniting our
resources, and by pooling our wits, we were
able to reach the outer world by the very agency
that was intended to obstruct us. The officers
of course knew this, but they were powerless.
And therefore, since accurate accounts of our
treatment were getting out to correct the
pleasing accounts published by the military,
the authorities, in their desire to conciliate
public opinion, were slowly compelled to make
their treatment square with their accounts,
just as they were being slowly compelled to
terminate the courtsmartial that hung over
the barracks, and seemed likely to last for
another year.

Our day began with the Reveille at six, and
concluded with Lights Out, at a quarter past
ten. The intervening hours were spent in
walking up and down the room and in talk.
The only thing that broke the monotony of the
day was the continuous business of the clearing-
house. Large batches of prisoners continued
to arrive from all parts of the country, where
the police were making hay while the sun shone,
to the no small embarrassment of the military,
who seemed likely to have the greater part of
the country delivered upon them. Large

batches were being deported to England ; and
there is no doubt that many were deported whom
the military had destined for their courts simply
because it had become impossible to warehouse
the cargoes of humanity that were being landed
on their wharf. And, in slowly diminishing
numbers, men were being selected . . . .
. . . . . . In the midst of this we lived
suspended until our turn came on the schedules
of the military wharfingers.

XI.

The day on which deportations were due was always tense and strained throughout. We were generally warned a day or so in advance by the soldiers, and sometimes had some of the names conveyed to us of those who were destined to go. However they obtained this information, it was always correct. This meant that from the time we awoke we were all restless. About two o'clock an officer would enter and read a list of names. Each of those so summoned would be given a knapsack, and informed that he was to be ready to fall in on parade outside at half-past two. No more was said ; and no more was needed to be said.

Some were glad to go. It meant their removal from the danger zone, and implied that the military did not know all that might have been known. But these were few. For the most part men waited anxiously all day, and if their names were called they made a brief comment, jocular sometimes, and sometimes defiant, that intimated the dead weight that had fallen on them with the news. Whatever courts-martial might sit, so long as we were in Ireland we were at home. There was always the consciousness with us that our own people were about us and bitterly resented our fate. Whereas deportation was deportation. Moreover, one of the men who had been deported a short time before had been brought back again for trial, and his tale of what had been meted out to him in an English jail was not pleasant to hear. Altogether, this breaking up of bonds and transference to the conqueror's own particular prisons was a thing of dread, however that dread might be covered by jocularity or grimness.

The first deportation after my arrival was on Saturday, May 20th. On that occasion none was taken from our room. We crowded to the windows to see the parade and to cheer our comrades by our presence there; but we were shouted back by the officers, who were conducting the parade,

.   .   .   .

Our very friendship with one another had become an offence.

The following week there was another list
of deportations. Three from our room were
taken, their places being filled the following
day by new arrivals from the country. On
May 23rd my name was called, with three
others from the room. The previous day I
had had an interview with solicitor and counsel
with a view to getting a statement of the charges
against me and to demanding a trial. An officer
had been present throughout the interview,
although we had protested against his presence.
He was under discipline to the very men against
whom it was our intention to proceed, and it
was a strange thing that he should be present
to learn exactly what our case might be and
how it was our intention to proceed. A further
interview was arranged for two days later, in
order that counsel might turn up certain points
of law. But in the meantime I received notice
that I was to be deported.

I had been, and then was, ill. I was really
unfit to travel, especially under these particular conditions. But that was a matter easily
mended. When I reported sick on parade I was
taken over to the dispensary and .   .   .   .   .
.   .   .   . Others who had
been summoned to the parade were treated in

the same way ; and we stood out there till about half-past four, when our escort arrived. It was a beautiful afternoon ; the sunlight poured down through a cloudless sky and lay like a sultry blanket on the ground. There were about a hundred and fifty of us, in two companies, for two destinations. We stood there in ranks with soldiers guarding us, while officers busied themselves with papers all about us. I thought of the sun shining on the sea, and clothing the mountains with a new soft beauty, and of the summer that began now to flow back over the earth in Achill. There was time to indulge in reflection to the full.

At five o'clock our guards handed us over to the escort. The barrack guard had been comprised of English troops. The escort was an Irish regiment. Ironic, that an Irish regiment should escort Irishmen for deportation to England. Stranger still when, as we were being marched through the city, the people crowded about us to let us know of their sympathy, and the soldiers were instructed to keep the people back with their rifle-stocks.

.   .   .   .   .   .

We are sometimes derided as a people rent by divisions, but the division in this case was due to the same cause as has created nearly all our other divisions. That cause was symbolised by the scene that was enacted that day. In no way more picturesquely could the fact of a perpetual military conquest have been staged. And when, as we marched down along the quays, most of us saw, for the first time, the havoc wrought in our capital by the guns of the conqueror, that only gave the appropriate scenery without which dramatists have agreed that the work of their artistry cannot be given to the world.

At the North Wall we were put on board a cattle boat. The cattle were herded at one end of the pens, we were being herded at the other end of the pens. When it came to my turn to be penned I was surprised to hear myself accosted by the Embarkation Officer :

" I'm B——, you know."

" Certainly, I replied ; " we meet again." But I had not the dimmest notion who he was.

" I hope to be in Castlebar soon," he said. " I haven't been back since I went out."

" Is that so ?" I said. "I was in Castlebar a fortnight ago. I was stopping at the jail."

He laughed, and turned to P. J. D., who stood beside me as we awaited our turn to be penned. His manner was frank and pleasant and not at all constrained, although his penning of us was quite efficiently done. I informed him that I was not well, and asked if certain accommodation could not be found slightly more efficient than a cattle pen packed with my fellows. He promised to see what he could do, and went off. When he had gone, P. J. D. informed me that he had been a Volunteer when I was in command of the county, and had since gained some distinction in the European War. Presently he returned, and conveyed some of us to a room in the forecastle, where we had seats on which we could stretch ourselves.

When we arrived in England, however, we struck quite another atmosphere. Inquisitive crowds gathered about us who lost no opportunity of displaying their enmity and hostility. German prisoners of war might have aroused an equal curiosity, but they could not have an equal enmity. Clearly and sharply we stood out, whether we gathered on railway platforms or were marched through streets, as nation against nation, with an unbridgeable hatred

F

between us.   Any attempt on our part to meet
taunt with taunt was at

.   .   .   .

; and so we were compelled to stand as
the mark of contumely and the target of con-
tempt.   To be sure, that only stiffened us, and
we held ourselves high and unflinchingly before
the crowds.   Nevertheless, there was a sickening
in most of us, for Ireland was behind us and we
were utterly in the stranger's power.

I had lived some years in England, and had
formed many good friendships.   Unlike many
of my companions, England and the English
were no strange things to me.   Yet I came
then into something utterly strange, foreign,
and hostile.   I could not more strangely have
been led captive among the mountains of the
moon, so icy was this world and such leagues
apart from that which I had known.

Everything was coloured by that relation.
One looked on England with new eyes, and old
thoughts became startling new discoveries.
Stafford lay for the most part steeped in slumber
as we were marched through its streets in the
morning, accompanied by ·a small, inquisitive
crowd.   It looked incredibly sleek and pros-

perous beside our Irish towns. The villas were
sleek and comfortable ; the roads were sleek
and neat ; the very grass beside the canal looked
sleek as though nurtured with the centuries.
Everything had an air of being well fed and
well groomed, and quite consciously proud of
the fact that it was part of a prosperous whole,
where no invader's foot had trampled, where no
spoliation had dared to efface the moss that had
gathered for centuries on the gables, or to rough
the smooth lawns. The villas might be the latest
examples of modernity, yet that was the air
they suggested, for they became part of something that was smooth and sleek. How different
to our Irish towns, that look as though they—
not the people in them, but they themselves—
live a precarious day-to-day existence. Each
suggests the history of their nation. One has
grown sleek with prosperity, and smooth and
round with the large air of the conqueror, with
shores that have never known invasion. The
other has been hunted from end to end by rapa-
cious conquest ; the forests that were its pride
burnt away the better to root out its people ;
the people hunted until they lost the instinct
to build for themselves permanent abodes, and,
more latterly, rack-rented till they stealthily

hid any small savings and kept middens before their doors, until a show of poverty from being a disguise became a habit ; rising against the conqueror in a series of revolts foredoomed to failure, but triumphant in what they spoke of— a spirit still unbroken ; stricken to earth again by soldiery that marched through the land ; and harnessed by a network of legislative acts that intended to inhibit industry and commerce with the nations of the earth, and that succeeded in their intention. And yet there was no question of a choice between the two. For with one individuality had become smoothened away, the wheel having come full circle ; with the other individuality was sharp and keen, angular it might be, but alive for the future.

H. P. and I were speaking of these things when we arrived at Stafford Jail. It was about six o'clock in the morning as we were marched through the gates and lined up outside the prison. The building looked gloomy and forbidding as it frowned down on us with its hundreds of barred windows. It had lately been used as a detention barracks ; that is to say, as a prison for soldiers, the major part of the population of England having donned khaki but not having doffed their sins therewith. Therefore, it was staffed by military, who received us from our escort and marched us up the great building to the cells that had been allotted us. And once again I heard the key grate behind me.

XII.

Stafford Jail covers a large space of ground surrounded by high brick walls, and contains three prisons, with the usual outhouses, such as the Governor's office, the reception-cells, the cookhouse, laundry, hospital, workshops, and chapels. In the centre stands the original prison, known as the Old Prison, a building of an old type of architecture, with high gabled roof and large windows. A path ran beside it, between it and the Governor's office, and this path led at each end to the two newer buildings that face each other and complete the square. One is known as the New Prison, of menacing exterior, with small windows heavily barred. The other is known as the Crescent, because of its shape. Both are plain solid buildings, but in the Crescent the windows are larger and less dungeon-like. Windows mean much to the outward look of a prison, but they mean much more to its inward life.

In the ordinary life of the jail—if it is at all possible to speak of a jail containing an ordinary life—women occupy the Old Prison, long-sentence and penal servitude men the New Prison, and short-sentence men the Crescent. While we were there soldiers under sentence occupied the Old Prison, and the Irish Prisoners of War the other two prisons. Dublin men occupied the Crescent, having been brought there on Monday, immediately after the surrender ; and the men from the country districts were put into the New Prison as they came to hand, together with a few Dublin men who had been swept up during the week after the Rising.

Flanking the jail on each side are the Union and the Lunatic Asylum, and to judge from the size of all three, the population of that part of England seems to be in a bad way. Afterwards I had an opportunity of looking from one of the higher windows over the walls, and I could see factory chimneys stretching to the horizon. Factory chimneys, lunatic asylums, jails, poorhouses, and sleek suburbia : a pretty picture of civilization. All the jail buildings were in red brick, which was at least warm to the eye. The New Prison held about four hundred cells, and the Crescent about the same.

Being one of the later Sweep-up I was placed in the New Prison. Within, it was not unlike a church in some ways, chiefly in the matter of gloom. It was comprised of three wings, branching from the central hall. Right and left ran a long high hall, with church-like windows at each end. Each side formed a wing, and opposite the gate there extended a third smaller wing. The walls of each wing rose like a cliff on either hand, with three tiers of cells like so many caves. Round the cells run balconies with spiral stairways connecting them. Across the midmost balcony wire netting is extended lest men's nerves get the better of them. Half-way down each wing the monotonous succession of cell doors is broken on each side, and a little recess formed for latrines.

Each wing bears a letter of the alphabet, and each cell a number. Each man on entrance has his name inscribed on one side of a cardboard form, and his cell number on the other. This is placed in a wooden slot outside his cell. The name is turned to the wall, and the number turned to view. By that is signified that his name is no longer needed, and he becomes a number. Inasmuch as the system is subtly devised for the extinction of personality, of identity, this is a deft piece of symbolism of which any dramatist might be proud. In Stafford I was C 2:21 :—Wing C., Balcony 2, Cell 21.

Cells are ever the same, even as their occupants are presumed to be. My cell at Stafford was the same as at Castlebar, save that the upper half of the walls was painted yellow instead of being whitewashed, the lower half red instead of yellow, and the floor paved. The window was much smaller and very dark. Unlike Castlebar, it had no gas jet inside. Instead of this, a square thick pane of glass beside the door covered an incandescent burner that was lit from outside. The cavity in which the burner stood narrowed to a small slit in the outer wall, lest any prisoner should magically narrow himself with a view to escaping through an aperture a foot square. Beside the door appeared the usual bell handle. By turning it sharply to one side a gong was rung above the latrine recess, and the same action registered one's number outside.

.   .   .   .

XIII.

All that I had feared in Castlebar now returned upon me ; yet, curiously, not so keenly, not so sharply. Already there had been a dulling of consciousness, a blunting of the susceptibilities. During the early morning we were examined medically and then bathed in antiseptic. We needed it ; herded on the dusty floors of Richmond Barracks we had collected what was to be collected, and had, as a Tyrone lad put it, " grazed our cattle through-other " ; and the doctor nodded gravely over his inspection, like one who thought, " Well, this is the Irish nation: report has not spoken untruly of them." Then we were taken back to our cells. During the afternoon we were taken out for a quarter of an hour's exercise in silence round one of the yards at the back of the prison, and solemnly informed that if any attempt to communicate with one another were detected we would be removed to special punishment cells and fed on bread and water for a week. Back to our cells then until the following afternoon.

That was our life. We were awoken at five and brought out for lavatory parade. Soon after six breakfast was served out to us. This consisted of a tin mug of tea, a square lump of white bread, and a small piece of margarine. Inasmuch as the mug served for soup as well as for tea, and presumably the tea was decocted in the same vessel as the soup, there was a strong similarity of taste between the two. Nor was the fluid that reached us always very hot. We were not permitted either knife, fork or spoon. While we took our breakfast the staff retired to theirs, and the curiously deathly prison silence descended on the place. At a quarter to eight the staff returned with the jangling of many keys, and soon the shouts of commands rent the air. For we were now to scrub out our cells. On the ground floor each man had, in addition to his cell, to scrub a portion of the hall opposite his door. When this was accomplished, if the staff-sergeant had any general instructions to announce, or could by any means devise an occasion for instructions, we were put on parade in the hall to hear him discourse. The staff-sergeant had a Biblical gift of iteration without the Biblical music of phrase. Nor had he the faculty of disguising his repetitions. He had, however, a certain ornateness of expression which, though it was not exactly Biblical, succeeded in relieving the monotony of his discourse. If he had two simple announcements to make he occupied himself for half an hour with them, and with variations on them, striding up and down the line of us, shouting at the top of his voice, while his staff of non-commissioned officers stood amongst us to see that we gave due heed to what he said. He was an excellent man, however; and meant kindly.

Back then to our cells, where we sat till dinner. This was brought round (by orderlies appointed from among ourselves) at twelve. Dinner consisted of soup and a lump of white bread. The soup was contained in the same mug as the morning tea, and was, until one became accustomed to it, a strange looking spectacle. In the midst of it floated a lump of something that varied according to one's varying luck. If one were fortunate it was, mainly, meat; if one's luck were only fair, it consisted of fat, with streaks of lean bravely running through it; if one's luck were completely out, it was gristle, with bits of meat set in it like amethysts in quartz (and indeed the meat was illuminated by strange colours astonishingly like amethysts). Either the animals slain for our eating were curious beasts or my luck was badly out, for the succession of gristle that came to my turn was noteworthy. Afterwards I managed to smuggle out one of the islands that floated in my soup, and sent it entire to a member of the English Parliament, thinking the effect might be remarkable if it were thrown dramatically across the floor of the House, as Burke once threw a dagger. Two or three potatoes in their skins were served with the soup ; and the whole meal had to be manipulated with one's fingers. I became quite expert with the course of time in discovering where pieces of meat crouched in their layers of gristle and bringing them to the light of day with my forefinger. Yet often I decided that the meal was not worth the fatigue involved, and left it where it stood.

The afternoons served our scanty pleasure, for then we were taken out for exercise, which usually lasted twenty minutes to half an hour, and on some occasions longer, according to the pleasure of the sergeant in control. For the staff worked through the prisoners in batches through the day. How one looked forward to that glimpse of sky overhead, to that beat of the summer's sun on one's body. The yard was of great size as befitted the size of the prison, and was laid with ground clinkers, or some black earth of the nature of ashes, surrounded by a concrete path. There was no colour to be seen anywhere, save the red bricks of the gaol and the black floor of the yard. Yet the sky was blue overhead, and the sun was golden ; and though these things were plaintive in what they told of a summer passing in pomp elsewhere, yet their immediate gift made that half hour of the day the moment for which we lived during the 23½ hours' existence in a cell. Moreover, after a time I tried an experiment. I quietly stepped out of the file into the yard and began running easily within the circle that the others made about me. I saw the sergeant look at me, not quite knowing what to make of the innovation. Then another stepped out, and ran behind me ; and another, and yet another, till there was a string of half a dozen of us. Nothing was said the first day ; and the innovation once begun it was continued. Thus we had another event to which to look forward during the long hours.

At five came tea, which was a repetition of breakfast ; and then set in the hours we most dreaded. The staff went home at five, and silence settled down over the prison—a silence that was not broken till five the next morning. Now and then as the night watchman passed in his padded shoes I would hear the spy-hole slot being moved aside and would know that an eye was looking in upon me. Then the slot fell back again. The eye had passed on to the next cell. But all the time the silence was profound.

The lengthening day, with the altered hour, gave light till ten at night. That is to say, the customary twilight of the cell did not change to profound gloom and then to darkness till after that hour. That made the case worse, for one would not take refuge in sleep. It would be hard to say how many times I counted the number of bolts that studded the door, how many times I counted the number of bricks in each wall, how many times I measured the number of feet from end to end of the cell, from side to side, and from corner to corner. This was one's occupation for twenty-three hours out of the twenty-four, save for the time given to sleep, until one fell back on bitter blank staring ahead.

Sometimes, as though to make the silence still more oppressive, I heard one of the other prisoners somewhere down the prison break into a song. Then a harsh voice would loudly call on him to be quiet ; and silence would be supreme again. Already on my first day I had established friendly relations with my corporal. He was, I discovered, a London Irishman, and he happened to be more easily quickened to interest on that account. I asked him once what the other men did with their time, when he spied in upon them, thinking to find comfort for my hours in a more intelligent knowledge of the life that was silently proceeding around me.

" Most of them just sit on their stools and stare at the wall. It's horrible to see them. Lots of them are crying—some that you wouldn't think of. And a lot of them are praying, always praying. And that's worse, for things are not as bad as that. It makes me feel bad to see them."

I thought of Dame Quickly with her, " Now I, to comfort him, bid him a' should not think of God ; I hoped there was no need to trouble himself with any such thoughts yet," and smiled. But I wished I had not asked him my question.

Yet, strangely enough, the thing that I had feared with such horror in its coming at Castlebar did not quicken in me such fear now that it had settled upon me. The process had, as most processes do, brought its own rather ghastly relief. In Castlebar I had been keen and sensitive ; my mind had been quick to speed ahead and anticipate the approaching evil ; and that, if painful, was a preferable estate to this dead inertia, when the mind seemed hardly to have any existence in the body.

.   .   .   .

and I cannot wonder at it ; for often one would spring to one's feet and march up and down the cell in a mental excitement that was almost unendurable. Such times, when they came, came intolerably, for they came with diminishing frequency ; but the usual state was inertia. There was something of learned patience about it ; something of a reserve that waited its day ; but deeper set than these things was the blankness of being that it was the first duty of the whole system to achieve.

I tried, for instance, to bring before me the faces of those whom I knew, and to imagine what they might be doing as I thought of them. I sought, thus, to give myself a life in the life

G

that others were living ; but could I think of those lives, could I bring their faces before me ? It was not that they fled me. The mind simply would not rise to the effort. I tried to surrender myself to problems of thought that had fascinated me in the past, and to problems of being into which all life's meaning had been crowded. But at most the wheel only spun round, never gripping the metal ; and more often the wheel refused to move. The life within the cell was significantly told by the card outside : the name was turned to the wall, and only a number was turned to view. Prison cells are not dwellings, they are sepulchres.

So the days passed, one by one, while the summer rolled by outside. Even the will to fight seemed lost.

XIV.

Sunday brought relief. That day there was no exercise ; but when we were aroused we all went to Mass. The Protestant Chapel was used, for there was no room elsewhere for both prisons-full. Everybody went, whatever our creed, both for the comfort of one another, and for the joint comfort of worship. There I saw for the first time the Dublin men from the Crescent, many of them known to me, many of them wearing the uniform of the Republican Army, in some cases scarred by battle. It was a large concourse, and the body of song was a joy to hear after our enforced silence. The warders sat at regular intervals on seats above us, with their backs turned to the Altar and their faces toward us, like strange idols perched aloft.

The priest, I learned, had told the first men on their arrival that he was there to fulfil his functions only, though he abhorred their actions and could have no dealings with them. This he had announced at their first Mass, and he had till now preserved that attitude, never suffering himself to discover by closer contact the cause of the sufferings that stirred his anger.

The following day I put myself down to see him, and during the course of the morning he visited me.

" You wish to see me," he said. He was exceedingly kind and courteous.

" Yes," I said ; " I wish to congratulate you on the fact that you are not here in prison with us."

" I don't understand you."

" For preaching sedition, or at least reading seditionary stuff. You recall the epistle you read yesterday ? I think it was misapplied, mind you. You were exhorting us to do just what we had done, and had been thrown into prison for ; but you read it all the same, and deserve congratulation. Do you remember :

' Be ye doers of the Word, and not hearers only, deceiving your own selves, for if a man be a hearer of the Word, and not a doer, he shall be compared to a man beholding his own countenance in a glass. For he beheld himself, and went his way, and presently forgot what manner of man he was. But he that hath looked into the perfect law of liberty, and hath continued therein, not becoming a forgetful hearer, but a doer of the work ; this man shall be blessed in his deed.'

" That's sound talk ; every word of it applies ; and we are blessed in the deed, though we are in prison all the same.

.   .   .   .

In that connection you think over that phrase about the man who looked into a mirror, and presently forgot what manner of man he was, till he became a doer of the Word after having looked into the perfect law of liberty. I thank you for that epistle ; and I congratulate you that you are not in prison."

Afterwards he moved among us intimately and always. He made it his business to know each man personally, and there was scarcely a man to whom he did not endear himself. In very literal truth he spent himself and his substance for us all. He got into touch with the men's families at home, and reassured both man and family as to the state of the other. During those days, indeed, he lived his life with

us, and every man turned to him as to a brother.
What he said to me of his opinion of the men
may pass; but I subsequently heard that he
said publicly in his chapel in the town that if
his hearers wished to know what faith was, what
religion, what principle and truth, he would
commend them to look in the jail.   He had his
convictions and emotions as an Englishman;
we had ours as Irishmen; but there is no man
who was at Stafford Jail for his convictions and
emotions who does not cherish with affection
the name of Father Moore.

Some Sundays afterwards he had occasion to
read the following epistle :—

> " Be you humbled under the mighty
> hand of God, that He may exalt you in the
> time of visitation.   Casting all your care
> upon Him, for He hath care of you.   Be
> sober and watch; for your adversary the
> devil, as a roaring lion goeth about, seeking
> whom he may devour; whom resist ye,
> strong in faith . . . "

As he did so, his eye travelled over to me; and
the following day he came over to me.

" I know what you are going to say.   You
make me watchful of my epistles," he said.

XV.

Deadened and inert though the barbarity of solitary confinement caused one to become (and even as solitary confinement ours was particularly severe and therefore particularly barbarous) there were times when the whole being rose in revolt. Anything would have been preferable to it. On one such occasion I demanded to see the Commandant of the jail. When he came, I requested to know exactly why I was being punished, and for what offence. I told him that I wished to have his answer in writing and to be able to communicate with my solicitor with a view to taking action. My thought was that a personal suit against him might prove abortive, but that it might cause a publicity the effect of which would be healthy.

He replied that I was not being punished ; that I was simply being " detained." I said that this could not be. According to prison regulations, solitary confinement of so severe a

nature was punishment at least equivalent to
birching. Would he birch me without acquaint-
ing me with the cause of such a punishment ?
No, he said, he would not. Then why, I asked,
was I receiving a punishment equivalent in
severity without a cause assigned. I wished to
be provided with a cause, and to be provided
with it in writing.

The Commandant himself was gentlemanly
and courteous. A few days afterwards when I
repeated my request he told me he was simply
acting under orders, and that he could not
change matters without orders. I asked him
then if he would communicate my request to
the War Office, under whose instructions he
proceeded ; and he promised to do so.

Some time elapsed ; and when he spoke to
me further about the matter he asked what it
was that I demanded. He asked me if I would
particularise. I replied that the War Office
had on their own initiative defined us as Prisoners of War. It had been announced to us that
all our letters had to be so addressed ; all the
orders given to us were made applicable under
that heading. I said I did not quarrel with the
designation ; both nationally and personally
I hailed it. It was, I agreed, a splendid desig-

nation ; but such being our state, I demanded on our behalf the application of the international agreement governing the treatment of prisoners of war—an agreement that, I believed, had been ratified between the belligerent powers during the first week of the war. In other words, I wanted tobacco and pipe, I wished any books that I might order or that might be sent in to me, daily papers, free communication with my fellow-prisoners, and the opening of cell doors by night and by day, the right to have food sent into us, and the return of my money in order that I might be able to purchase food in the town, and facilities to purchase it, by canteen or by order. I added that what I demanded I demanded not for myself but for all of us, and in all of the prisons.

After a few days he came to me to say that the War Office had authorised him to grant these rights, but to grant them in stages, and with one stipulation. That stipulation he would announce to the men. Having put us all on parade he announced the rights that would be granted, but said that it would first be necessary for us to choose a commandant from among ourselves who would be responsible to him for the good order of the prison, and who would have power to maintain discipline. The men appointed me, and I created officers for each of the landings.

So began our little republic, and so extended our educative influence. When the rights were in full force the staff became supernumeraries We created our post office and handled our own parcels and letters for distribution. Rules were laid down for the ordering of our life together ; and only once or twice was it necessary to take disciplinary measures (solitary confinement in one case as a pathetic reminder !), for the general spirit of loyalty and affection was sufficient—was, in fact, remarkable with a body of men not accustomed to the strict rules necessary to the ordering of such a community. The appointed officers were responsible for their landings, made daily reports, and brought up any cases with which they were unable to deal. And so from top to bottom we maintained ourselves, quietly eliminating the staff, to the no small dissatisfaction of some of them, though with the good will of most. There was, in fact, no work for most of the staff to do.

At seven each morning, after breakfast, and at eight at night, the bell was rung, and we all gathered for public prayers. Michael MacRory,

Irish orator, and Padraic Pearse's gardener, led the Rosary. Englishmen speak much of our religious differences. It devolved upon me as a Protestant to summon the prayers, and none thought otherwise of it than as a natural thing, while every Protestant knelt with his fellows in prayer to the one God. Whatever announcements or enquiries Father Moore had to make were made through a Protestant, and had anyone suggested that they should not have been so made, it would have fared ill with him. They were made as a simple matter of authority by whoever was in authority. The reason for this was that we were sufficient in ourselves to guard over our own affairs without a stranger's hand to create trouble.

These daily prayers were a great astonishment to the staff. One sergeant declared to a visitor : " I heard a lot about these Sinn Feiners being a bad lot, but you should see them. They're a religious lot. They goes to prayers and church same as we goes to the theaytre." And when, some days after our public prayers had begun, the news came that the " Hampshire " had sunk, there was not a man of the staff but was fully assured that it was our prayers had sent Lord Kitchener to his death.

At ten each night every man was required to be off the corridor and balconies, and any conversation in cells after that time had to be conducted softly, in order not to interfere with those who wished to sleep; and within five minutes of the ringing of the bell the prison was clear and quiet. The staff became accustomed, if they had business to execute with us, to resign it into our hands for prosecution. Those who did not do so made a sad affair of their undertaking. Which is a parable. In a phrase, our motto was: Sinn Féin Amáin.

It was interesting to notice our influence on the staff. We never troubled about them; they had their interests and we had ours; and only occasionally the national opposition clashed sharply. Yet they confided in us. With our extended rights the library was opened to us; and the librarian-warder informed us that he was at first afraid to be left alone in the library with any one of us. Apparently he thought we would bite out his windpipe unexpectedly, or playfully split his skull. But when his first visitor, a man from Belfast, contemptuously described his collection of books as "piffle," and asked that certain other books should be procured from the officers' library, as he himself declared : " My word, I was surprised. I thought you Sinn Feiners were a wild lot of savages from what I heard of you. But you are men of culture, most of you. It's a bit of a shock to a man to find out." The librarian-warder was quite pleased at the widening range of his ethnographical knowledge.

Yet the most interesting member of the staff was the sergeant of the R.A.M.C. He was a Doctor of Literature at Oxford, and also, I believe, a *Docteur ès Lettres* at the Sorbonne. He had been out at Gallipoli, whence he had been invalided home. As he passed on his rounds he would often come into my cell for a talk. We very seldom spoke on national questions, for I assumed that our orbits of interest on such matters would not cut each other at any point ; our conversation was generally on literary or philosophical matters. But once he came up to me with a definite thing to say.

" You know," he said, " the Government make a great mistake putting men like you into prison. You will never forget it ; you can never forget it ; no man could who canvasses experience with his intellect. They're simply a lot of grandfatherly old fools at the top of affairs, and we always make a muddle of things.

They should either give you a clear run, and let you make what you can of your country and take the chances ; or they should wait their chance and shoot you out of hand and laugh at the racket afterwards. But all this sentimental talk about your country, followed up by all this muddle, simply makes a thinking man sick. All this business," and he indicated the hundreds of us standing talking about the yard, " is clumsy, it's idiocy, and it breeds more clumsiness and idiocy for the future."

" Which of your two alternatives would you adopt ? " I asked him.

" Well, you know, one likes to meet a man to whom one can talk ; intellect, and all that sort of thing, and culture, and care for art, they're rare enough in this world, and one wouldn't altogether care to take the responsibility of destroying any part of it —— "

" But you'd shoot me all the same."

" Yes, I think I would." He was quite serious. " Quite possibly that's because I've just been seeing a lot of blood ; and I don't think I would have said that two years ago. But just now I'd shoot you. I wouldn't of course do it in a stupid way. I'd wait till you gave me a chance ; and sooner or later you would, for you have your convictions, and they'd lead you into my hand ; and then I'd shoot you instantly, and without trial if need be, without waiting anyhow. Of course there'd be trouble afterwards, but I'd wait quietly till that blew over, as it would."

" That wouldn't get you out of the wood, for you'd make a martyr of me and exploit my ideals."

" That's so. There's that side, of course. But still that's what I think I'd do. I certainly wouldn't go muddling about trying to do two mutually contradictory things at the same time. All you men here—the whole thing's simply offensive."

" Does the hypocrisy offend you then ? You ought to have become accustomed to that by this time as a nation."

" Well, yes, in a way it does, I suppose. But it's not that mainly ; it's the clumsy thinking ; it's not thinking the thing out from the beginning. Do I horrify you ? "

" Not at all. If you came over to Ireland you'd have a great audience. We'd agree with you in every word, simply and utterly. We'd be delighted to meet one of your nation who looked at things without any silly sentiment. You're

a sentimental people, and at bottom very cruel ;
we're not sentimental. You are as sentimental
as any yourself ; but you've at least got your
mentality clear of it, and so for the first time
you can see things as they are. The worst
of it is that, dealing with a sentimental people,
you are making us superficially sentimental
too, and that's distracting us from our work.
I only wish that more of you would talk as you
do, instead of slobbering. And shoot away ;
as long as you say why, without using words
that convey nothing to us and that only mean
sloppy thinking on your part."

" But I thought you objected to the shootings
in Dublin."

" Certainly. Those men were my brothers.
But they weren't shot as you said you'd shoot
me, because you were out to smash an opposed
thing as the only logical alternative to giving
it the run of its own life, but, if you please,
because they didn't accept certain standards
which none of us can ever accept until we make
and endorse them in terms of ourselves—or,
rather, which we now do and must for ever
act upon in that sense, because it's the first
principle of life so to do. And then, when you
have them shot, you turn round and praise their

noble ideals ! In the name of heaven, what ideals ? "

" I think I should certainly shoot you now."

" To smash me. Good man ! We'd understand that in Ireland, where your Liberal sentiments bore us, and your Tory hectoring irritates us. We're a kindly people—human and hospitable ; but you, because you can escape into words and hide realities from yourselves, are cruel and inhospitable."

And I believe he would have shot me. Many were the conversations we had ; many were the kindly, thoughtful acts he did for us ; and he was courtesy itself to the ladies who spent their days at the prison gate taking rebuffs from everyone in the prison, in the determination to see that each man of us received what he had need of, food or clothing. But he would have reasoned the thing out and shot me, without the least ill-will or high-falutin. And I would have borne him no ill-will, for the fight would have continued long past the two of us.

XVI.

These more fortunate times soon came to an end—for me at least. So long as they lasted they were not intolerable ; and the various funds in aid of prisoners, and the companies of our fellow-countrymen and women (chiefly women !) who came to visit us, made captivity as amenable as it could be made. But one morning I was summoned to the Commandant's office, and informed that I and some fifty others were to be sent that day to an internment camp at Frongoch in Wales. We were to be the first to arrive, and we were to take charge of the camp and order and regulate it for the remainder of the Irish Prisoners of War, who would arrive in detachments from Stafford, from Knutsford, from Perth, from Glasgow, from Wakefield, from Wandsworth, and from Lewes.

Such were the orders, and we were to be ready to leave in an hour's time. But I had what

H. P. afterwards chaffingly alluded to as my
" strategic illness." Never till then did I
admire the amazing insight and foresight of
Dublin Castle.

.   .   .   .

I was in fact covered from head to foot with
the proof of their perspicuity.   And as a result
all the detachments to Frongoch from Stafford
were held back for three weeks to cover the
period of infection.

Thus I spent nearly a fortnight in hospital
in the company of an R.A.M.C. corporal who was
isolated with me.   He had been a Northumber-
land mines inspector, and we discussed the
working of mines, their proprietorship and
profits, and the virtues of Trades Unions.   Sometimes my friend the sergeant came and stood
out of sight, and beyond infection, behind the
door.   He informed me that it had been discovered that I had written a book on Shakespeare, and that I was to be treated with respect accordingly.   He seemed to be somewhat
amused at this.   But my corporal snorted with
northern scorn, and declared that if I could not
be treated with respect as a man, I should not

be treated with respect as a man who had written books. So, with one hand, one touched both ends of English society.

When I rose I was informed by the Commandant that I was not to rejoin the others. Since I had been ill, it appeared, instructions had been received that I and another were to be isolated. That other (H. P.) was already in a cell in the Crescent, where I was to be taken. He and I would be allowed to speak to one another whenever the staff arrangements permitted of it ; but never, under any circumstances, were we to be allowed to communicate with the others. And, at the same time, he handed me my official order of internment, stating that according to regulations drafted for dealing with " aliens," I was to be interned because I was " reasonably suspected of having favoured, promoted or assisted an armed insurrection against His Majesty."

It was easy to see a craftier hand than that of the War Office at work in this. Yet, by isolating us they magnified us : a result, indeed, that the smallest wit could have foreseen. We were exercised together in the afternoon ; and when, the first day, we passed within sight of the others they hailed us unitedly from the distance.

Thereafter we were not permitted to pass within sight of them.

The rooms into which we had been put had been designed for consumptive prisoners, and contained bracket beds attached to the wall. The walls were plastered and smooth, and painted in a pleasing combination of two greens. Little things ; but what they meant to anyone who had to spend his day sitting in a small cell ! What chiefly delighted me, however, was the blanket on my bed. It would have given joy to a Red Indian chief. Its colours were green, claret, and yellow. It lay on my bed like a spread cockatoo. Life could not be drab with that to look upon. Moreover, I had books, and I was allowed foolscap on which to write. So with books, pen and blanket, the days passed with as much ease as a prison could give. For, strangely enough, though the severity of our condition had been much relaxed, the presence and the effect of the system remained. Books that demanded any thought in the reading were avoided ; the mind seemed incapable of the effort they demanded ; as soon as a page were read it passed from the memory, and the mind became once again a blank. One rebelled against this at first, and sought to conquer it ;

but when the will demanded an effort, the brain replied that such efforts were for another, not for this world, that the soul could not realise itself in a world that had been wrought as nearly as possible to resemble a vacuum.

A sergeant had been placed in charge of the two of us, a grown child of a man, with all a child's shrewdness and sharpness, and from him we received many friendly acts in spite of the fact that he seemed constantly to live in fear of some judgment that would alight on him. He would take me into H. P.'s cell for conversation, and he came to the tolling of the gong without a murmur or complaint. And for twenty minutes each day I saw my wife at the iron gate—who, in truth, lived her days at that gate.

Then one day Father Moore came into my room and sat on my bed, with the tears in his eyes. "They're taking the men away from me," he said. The dear man was heart-sore at the parting that now began. Every few days saw the men leaving in batches of fifty to a hundred on their way to Frongoch. Sometimes from a distance we could see them going. More often we had to rely on news brought us from our sergeant. The final stage of our journey was to begin ; for we nothing doubted that our destination was to be the same as theirs—Frongoch, from which place no good reports came.

It was not till they had all gone, and we had had the long desolate prison to ourselves for over a week that we were informed that we were not to go to Frongoch, but were to be removed to Reading Jail. The others having gone, and the fear of our contamination removed, we had been permitted the run of the prison ; and quite probably we were the only prisoners in all time who paced alone a long prison that echoed to our steps. The effluence of many thousands of prisoners was about us ; and we entered the cells to find the names they had scratched and to reconstruct their history.

Then one morning, July 10th, we were marched out under yet another sergeant's guard for Reading Jail.

XVIII.

Reading Jail that day was a mustering of the clans. All the isolation men from the various prisons, Wakefield, Knutsford, and Wandsworth, including many who had been to Frongoch, were gathered together at Reading. It was meant as an elect company ; but it was not at all as elect as the selectors imagined. We ourselves entertained no delusions on that head. One of the most distinguished of our company had been wildly hailed on his arrival months before at Wandsworth, as the man who " 'ad been a-hinciting of 'em " ; and apparently the net had been thrown to sweep into Reading all those who " 'ad been a-hinciting of 'em " ; but the net had had a singularly faulty mesh. Even the original net that had swept through the country during the month of May, carefully though it had been wrought, and thoroughly though it had been cast, had had a mesh none too perfect. There were but twenty-eight of us gathered together that day ; and we had, as it were, a double crown pressed on our heads ; but we made haste to disown the title to wear it.

Yet we were glad to meet. National work necessarily intersects at many points, and so most' of us who foregathered that day for our months of association had met before in differing combinations, and at different times, in differing groups of work that were but part of the one great work. Yet we had never met in that particular combination before. Some came representing the leadership of large districts, counties or cities, and some represented national leadership from some more central focus. The provinces were indeed as nearly represented as they could well be : eight came from Connacht, seven from Leinster, seven from Munster, and six from Ulster ; or, fourteen from Leth Chuinn and fourteen from Leth Mhogha. It was exceedingly well arranged. Though we were not as complete as we might have been, though we did not venture to conceive of ourselves as an assembly either inclusive or exclusive of anything, yet the general representation was very evenly matched. And it was yet more evenly when, two days later, another Ulster repre-

sentative arrived ; for, as it so fell out, a
Connacht man had been elected as Ceannphort,
and so the provinces were left matched with a
perfect seven apiece.

Such was the skill the Government of England
had taken to see, not only that we had an
opportunity of meeting and understanding one
another such as we never could have hoped for,
but that we should meet as a well-balanced and
proportionate whole. The care with which this
was wrought must have been considerable.

The only drawback to our assembly was the
uncertainty of date when we discontinue it, and
the building in which we met.

XVIII.

Reading, being set deep in a valley at the confluence of two rivers, is an unhealthy town, close and sultry by summer, and damp and misty by winter. The gaol is a handsome building, erected in red brick after the manner of an old castle, with battlements and towers. One almost expected a portcullis to be lowered at the great gate ; and when we were within the double gates we certainly felt as though a portcullis had been drawn after us. We stood in a small cobbled yard. Behind us was the broad wall in which the double gates were set, flanked on each side by the Governor's and the Steward's houses. Before us a flight of stone steps arose, leading to the offices, behind which was the large male prison. To the right a wall arose dividing us from the work yard ; and on the left a high blind wall arose, pierced only by a single door near the wall round the jail. This was the female prison—ordinarily so, but for the time being our habitation.

Yet what astonished me most was the sight of
flowers. Their presence made the cobbled yard
and the precincts seem almost collegiate. In
neatly kept beds about the walls they lifted their
heads with a happy gaiety very strange to some
of us who had known so human a touch banished
from buildings more appropriately given over
to the possession of flints and cinders. A few
days after we were taken through the work
yard behind the main prison. Here in the work
hall a canteen was opened on three days in the
week for the interned prisoners who now
occupied the prison, but here also was the large
exercise yard, and it was covered with an abun-
dance of flowers. The familiar asphalt paths
could not be seen where they threaded their
way amid blossoms. In beds beneath the walls
tall flowers lifted their heads, and even the graves
of hanged men could not be seen beneath the
blooms that covered them.

It was an amazing sight. There were not
merely flowers, a sight astonishing enough in
itself ; there was a prodigality of flowers. Then
some of us remembered the cause. One of the
graves unlocked the secret. It was marked
with the letters C. T. W., and the date, 1896,
to whom Oscar Wilde's " Ballad of Reading

Jail " had been inscribed, and in celebration of
whose passing the poem had been penned.

> But neither milk-white rose nor red
>   May bloom in prison-air ;
> The shard, the pebble, and the flint
>   Are what they give us there :
> For flowers have been known to heal
>   A common man's despair.

> So never will wine-red rose or white
>   Petal by petal, fall
> On that stretch of mud and sand that lies
>   By the hideous prison-wall,
> To tell the men who tramp the yard
>   That God's Son died for all.

So Wilde had sung, not in protest, but in bitter
acceptance, never dreaming that a poet's song
could change the flint, the pebble, and the
shard of the yard he trod. But for us who
came after him with the memory of his song in
our minds, the miracle had been wrought.
Miracle it was, and it had been wrought in no
common sort, for the great yard was a lake
of leaf and bloom, and the hideous prison wall
was transformed by gay figures decked in

raiment that not Solomon in all his glory could outvie.

Already in the pebbled entrance yard the hand of this "unacknowledged legislator" was in evidence. We were first taken across to the office, as we arrived in batches, and our money taken from us, and our kit examined. Then we were led back through the door in the blind wall into the female prison, that had been allocated to Irish Prisoners of War. The main prison was occupied by the nations of Europe Belgians, Germans, French, Rumanians, Russians, and indeed every degree and variety of European to the number of fourteen.

.   .   .   .

The prison actually held only twenty-two cells. There were in addition a hospital, a maternity ward, and two padded cells, one permanent and one temporary. The hospital and maternity ward consisted of two cells each, with the intervening wall removed. In each of these three men were placed (there being some little rivalry for the maternity ward), which with the use of the temporary padded cell provided for all of us. In addition to this, there was also an observation ward, on the ground floor, similarly constructed of two cells converted into one, and this was given to us as a recreation room. All these cells were on one side of the building, the other side being a blank wall, and the only light that came to the passage struggled down through skylights.

Such was the place that was to be our habitation for nearly six months, and in which we erected the structure of our communal life.

XIX.

We had all come with experience of prison life, and were not easily perturbed. We had become accustomed to taking things as we found them, and making them the basis of improvement, not in the mood of those who sought privileges, but as those who demanded rights. Our first act was to elect a Ceann-Phort, through whom to formulate our demands, and by whom to lay out the lines of our life together. Our next act was to put together the tables that stood in the passage in order that we might have our meals together. From the very first during the time we were permitted together we at once took the control of our affairs into our own hands, and it became a recognised principle that any dealings of officials with us were with us as a whole and not with individuals.

For instance, the prison had to be scrubbed through twice a week, and in addition there was orderly work to be appointed, such as daily sweeping, polishing of rails, cleaning of dishes, and, as we had elected to take our meals together, the preparation and clearance of tables. For this work it was proposed, as in the usual way, to select the required men, and to pay them at the prison rate of ten pence a day. Instead of that we desired that the payment should be made to the Ceann-Phort, saying that the work would be done under his arrangements. We were then drawn out into eight teams who took it in turns for orderly work. The fatigues on Wednesday and Saturday were taken by each half-company of four teams. All questions concerning our life were arranged between our Ceann-Phort and the prison Governor.

The moneys that were paid over to us were expended by us, together with contributions made from time to time from among us, on the canteen that was open three days in the week. For the food that we received was the same as we had received in other prisons, except that at first its quality was improved. While our exchequers lasted we were able to enrich our dietary to some extent by extra doles of bread, margarine and sugar. This canteen was in the hands of one of the grocers in the town for the use of all the prisoners in the jail.

The first night we were locked up at eight o'clock, with lights out at nine. This was one of the first matters to which we turned our attention. We were not successful in approximating this to the conditions that had prevailed elsewhere with us, such as at Stafford, but we were finally able to have the time altered to ten. The gravest hardships, however, in the conditions as at first announced to us were that we were only suffered one visit every three months and one letter each month. These were the ordinary conditions imposed on penal servitude convicts,

.   .   .   .

Finally we were permitted one visit a month and two letters each week, the letters to be written on little slips of paper provided for us. At first also we were refused the right to receive parcels of food sent in by friends. This was clearly contrary to the code prevailing for Prisoners .   .   . ; and this also we had annulled.

Therefore our life, as finally adjusted, was on this wise. We were aroused at seven o'clock, and the orderlies for the day at once laid the breakfast, which was taken at a quarter to eight. At half-past ten we were taken out by the warders to the work yard for exercise.

There we disported ourselves as we pleased
until we were brought in for dinner at twelve.
In the afternoon we went out, not to the work
yard, but to the small exercise yard at the back
of our prison. This was separated by a wall
from the Debtors' Yard, of which Wilde had
sung :

> In Debtors' Yard the stones are hard,
>   And the dripping wall is high.

Then tea at five—

> And the bitter bread they weigh in scales
>   Is full of chalk and lime.

After tea, during the summer months, we were
allowed out into the yard again till it was
dark, and at ten the key grated against us once
more in our cell doors.

> Each narrow cell in which we dwell
>   Is a foul and dark latrine,
> And the fetid breath of living death
>   Chokes up each grated screen,
> And all, but Lust, is turned to dust
>   In Humanity's machine.

XX.

We were treading a path that had already
been sung (for even bitterness has its song)
but we trod it in greater comfort. Above all
we had one another's company. The boon of
this might conceivably have been blurred a
little, as with the passage of months it became
difficult in our cramped space to avoid treading
on one another's toes. And certainly it was
impossible for each man not to know each other
at his best and worst. The knowledge so gained
had its value for future days. For at bottom
the solidity with which we began was only
cemented with the passage of time.

Yet our company was first to be revised, by
a process of addition and subtraction, before
it took its final shape. One Friday in August
we were informed that on the Monday and
Tuesday following we were to be taken in two
parties before the Advisory Committee. We
were asked to give our word that we would

make no attempt to escape. If we gave that pledge we would be sent to London with warders in plain clothes ; otherwise it would be necessary to send us handcuffed together. On this a keen discussion took place; for while the majority was content to give the undertaking there were some who would give no pledge, who would leave it to the authorities to decide for themselves on any action they pleased. Finally the Governor, who was very anxious to avoid handcuffs, assumed an undertaking, and so the issue was muffled. Two warders in plain clothes accompanied each party to Wormwood Scrubbs Jail ; and nothing was done to advertise the fact that we were prisoners travelling. Had the question arisen a few months later hardly a man would have given the undertaking, or even have suffered it to be implied. The public display of handcuffs would have been coveted rather than avoided ; for it was certainly not to comfort us that the offer was made, whatever the Governor's personal inclinations might have been. For jails but straighten the back and harden the mind.

We also differed in our attitude towards the Advisory Committee. None of us differed in our opinion of its function. It sat, so the purport ran, to decide which of us might be liberated ; or rather, more technically, in respect of which of us our internment orders should be confirmed ; but these things, as we know, would be decided by political considerations quite outside the review of the Committee. None of us doubted that its main function was to check and complete our *Leabhrain*, as far as possible, by question and cross reference. But we differed in our attitude. Some refused to recognise the Committee in any way, as being a body set up by a foreign government, having no authority over Irishmen. These, when brought before the Committee, firmly defined their attitude, and were promptly escorted again into the outside air. Others answered the brief interrogatory to which they were submitted, and went their way in a matter of minutes. My own attitude was somewhat different.

In the first place, I had now been in prison for some months, without much chance of enlivenment. The opportunity of a debate through the labyrinth of the Defence of the Realm Regulations seemed too good a thing to be lightly put by. Moreover, I was anxious to discover some of the items that furnished my *leabhran*. I was not disappointed. As I had expected, deftly mixed among the questions put to me about my own doings were a number of questions that involved others. Also, as I had expected, a week's study of the Regulations left the rather interesting legal debate not altogether a one-sided matter ; for a number of points were conceded to me, which, when I afterwards sought to take advantage of them, proved to have been made without any deep knowledge of the possibilities the Regulations offered. One or two matters of interest emerged, however.

For instance, the Committee had some little difficulty in explaining exactly why, if I as an Irishman was to be interned as an

.   .   .   .

This, I was told, was a political matter. Strangely enough, it was exactly so I had conceived it. Then I was informed that I was only considered as an *alien* for the purposes of that particular act, that in other matters my citizenship under the law was not disputed. By which it appeared that I was an alien when my imprisonment was desired, but not an alien when my personal and national freedom was to be consulted.

Then, among other questions, I was asked if I had or had not endeavoured to get Irish farm labourers into touch with Irish farmers in order to stay their migrating to England, where they could be taken under the Military Service Act. On my asking on what authority the question was put, I was answered that it was so alleged in the local police report. My answer was an admission of the charge. I suggested that it might have a bearing that the assurance had been made in Parliament that farm labourers from Ireland could not be taken under the Military Service Act. But it was interesting to discover that a benefit intended to Ireland was made the basis of a charge ; and it was interesting to discover the furniture that found its way into police reports.*

When I came out and explained how it was I had remained so long, when all the others had been dispatched in two minutes or three, I was told that I had at least ensured continued internment. The price was not exhorbitant.

---

* It seems worthy of note that as I write in the year 1917 the Department of Agriculture and Technical Education have adopted this scheme, and are being assisted in its prosecution by the police. It took a Clown to refer to Time as a whirligig.

XXI.

The week after our excursion to Wormwood Scrubbs, seven men were sent down to us from Frongoch, where trouble had already begun. There were no cells to hold them in our prison, and so they were lodged in the reception-cells under the offices, where neither light nor air was bold enough to venture. They were brought over to us for breakfast, and lived during the day with us until they were taken back to bed.

Shortly afterwards five of our number were summoned to the Governor's office, and returned saying they were to be released that day. We already had had that joke played on us several times, and so we gave no heed to them. But when in a short time we saw them industriously packing their kit, the joke wore a more earnest expression. It was no jest, however. Although no man changed his mien yet none but felt what a jewel freedom was when it became within the grasp of his neighbour, and when that neighbour rose up and went forth proudly wearing it. We sang them home,' however, gaily enough. In a week two more were sent home. These seven comprised all the releases from Reading at the same time that two thousand and more were released from Frongoch. It was not very difficult to discover the reasons prompting most of these releases, and it need hardly be said that they had little relation to the events of Easter Week. The internments covered a much wider ground, which was chosen for much subtler reasons. The soldier's hand might rule in Ireland, but the politician's hand indexed the internments. And as usual the politician over-reached himself. For the men who were released found on their return that the country judged them unworthy to remain ; and the Home Office officials were finally convinced that Ireland was inhabited by the mad when they received shoals of letters from released men pitifully arguing that their releases must have been in error, and giving proofs of their part in the Rising-Out.

We, however, settled down to the honour of imprisonment with fortitude. Already, when we had learned that the celebrations of the 12th of July had been forbidden in Ulster we had filled the gap with a procession and a meeting in which excellent Orange speeches had been made.   Now we held a Hibernian meeting. Such things enlivened our days.

We suffered greatly from lack of exercise, and the closeness of our confinement began to tell upon us as the autumn approached.   We had given up going out to the work-yard for our morning exercise, and kept to the little yard. This yard was beset on three sides by the buildings of the jail, and on the fourth side, beyond the high wall, Huntley & Palmer's chimneys belched black smoke that blotted the sky.   In a corner of this yard we made a hand-ball alley.   No stranger alley was ever devised.   Two windows, a drain-pipe, a railing across steps leading to the basement, and a ventilator grating, gave opportunity for chance and skill.   And the exercise saved us.

Nevertheless, with the coming of winter the effects of our confinement could be seen on most of us.   The food, also, had become bad.   The margarine was often rancid.   On two occasions the meat made several of us ill ;   and for three months I lived only on bread and porridge, both of which were, at least, clean and wholesome. Prisons are not built as health resorts, yet precautions are supposed to be taken that a mean of temperature is maintained. During a week of frost, however, the temperature in my room was 46° to 48° Fahrenheit. This was inside the cells : outside, the passage was full of draughts. Yet the prison was never ventilated, for the only place where air could come or go was the door. The result was that when one of the warders came in once with influenza, every man in the prison in time fell to it.

Yet we kept our backs straight. P. J. D. was informed by the Governor, on the authority of the Home Office, that if he would sign an undertaking to be of good behaviour for the future he would at once be liberated. He replied that the offer was adding insult to injury, and he declared that if his liberation depended on his signature of any manner of undertaking, he was destined to remain long in prison. The Chief Warder approached others of us, thinking to try the ground before any other offers were made ; but he left matters as he found them.

In Frongoch at this time the same attitude was being taken. Matters there were also complicated by the attempt of the military to search out Irishmen who had returned home from England on the passage of the Military

Service Act—to search them out, not for the Army, but for the pleasure of thrusting them into jails.   And the result of the ensuing resistance was that seven of the leaders there were brought to Reading and put into the reception-cells, making our number thirty-five once again

XXII.

So the winter days passed. The prison was
wrapt continually in an unpleasant amalgam
of winter fog and Huntley & Palmer's smoke.
We never saw the sun, though occasionally,
when the fog cleared, we could make a guess
at it where it strode the sky.

Little wonder if we occasionally got upon one
another's nerves. None of our nerves were of
the best, and we all felt the deathly system of
prison life like an oppression on us, blotting out
all intellectual life and making a blank of mind
and soul. Yet no outsider saw cleavage among
us. That was a principle we never let down.

Of an evening we met together and discussed
different aspects of national affairs, partly with
the intention of defining our future action, and
partly with a view to defining our points of
view in their relation to one another. The two
things were really one; for satisfactorily to
outline the second was already largely to com-

plete the first ; and we were determined not to lose the chance with which we had been so admirably furnished. Moreover, when birthdays arrived we had modest supper-parties, in which song and good will supplied the lack of viands.

Yet towards the end, with illness and depression settling on most of us, we kept largely to our own cells, despite their icy temperature. We were suffered books—carefully selected. It became part of our business carefully to test the selection by arranging for a variety of books to be sent in to us by friends. Especially was this so when a happy accident gave us the name of our censor ; and it was deeply interesting to see his path among the classics of Irish literature.

In this we were assisted by our friends outside. Indeed, not the least value of our months of imprisonment was the revelation of friendship, and its spontaneity and strength and unity in those of our race. We had but to express a need and it was at once met by leagues and committees that had been gathered together, both at home and in England, to befriend and serve us. If our state was like that of an island it was at least an island washed by a great sea of friendship.

The gifts cast up by the tides of that sea became embarrassing as Christmas approached. We had altogether to dispense with prison fare ; and our thrills of excitement were not the less because we were so remote from the outer world. But the full bounty of that sea was never to be experienced by us.

Shut away though we were, we watched political affairs closely—watched not merely the surface that appeared, but watched for indications of the hidden streams that ran— and when John Dillon brought forward his motion for the discussion of the Irish Prisoners of War we guessed that he had learned some hint that we were to be released. This came soon after the failure to get us to sign pledges of good behaviour. When, however, the threatened motion was never taken, it was clear that we were not to be released. We were not greatly affected ; but we watched that pending motion with interest. It became a theme of daily jest with us. When, after the change of government, the motion at last was discussed, the sign was clear to us ; and we were not surprised when, the following day, we learned that Irish interned prisoners were to be released. In a non-committal way some of us began to pack—like

men who were content, the next moment, to
unpack, and take whatever came without per-
turbation. On Friday, the 22nd of December,
we heard that the Frongoch men were going, and
during that day we learned that a courier was
expected during the afternoon with papers for
our release. No courier, however, arrived ;
and Sunday saw us content again to continue
as we were without complaint. It appeared,
as I afterwards learnt, that the Home Office
had actually arranged for our release together
with the men at Frongoch, but that the Irish
Office had intervened. It was not till the
Sunday afternoon that the Home Office won its
way. For on that day, Christmas Eve, at half-
past two, the Governor came into the prison
to tell us that we were to be ready to go out in
two hours' time. It seemed indeed that our
maximum of inconvenience had been sought ;
for it was impossible then for many of us to reach
home for Christmas, and such men had need to
lodge where they could with the more fortunate.

So at half-past four we passed out through the
streets of Reading, singing our songs as we went.
Each man went to take up his duty as he had
always conceived it, but with the added hard-
ness inevitably begotten of a jail. And each

K

man remembered his fellows who still were in jail, the men who, for the same duty and for the same high cause, were serving sentences at Lewes, beside whom our sufferings were a light thing lightly endured.